ON T[...]L
SUMMIT

ON TO THE SUMMIT

THE
Len Moules
STORY

Pat Wraight

LITERATURE

P.O. Box 1047, 129 Mobilization Drive
Waynesboro, GA 30830-2047, U.S.A.

Copyright © Pat Wraight 1981

First published 1981
Reprinted 1981
Reprinted 1998

All rights reserved.
No part of this publication may be reproduced
or transmitted in any form or by any means, electronic
or mechanical, including photocopy, recording, or any
information storage and retrieval system, without
permission in writing from the publisher.

ISBN 1-884543-20-0

Published by OM Literature

OM Literature is a part of Operation Mobilization
P.O. Box 1047, Waynesboro, GA 30830-0028

Printed in Colombia
Impreso en Colombia

CONTENTS

ACKNOWLEDGEMENTS
AND THANKS

Thank you, Lord, for the privilege of writing this book

Thank you, friends, for sending tapes and letters from round the world

Thank you, WEC, for your help and encouragement

Thank you, Iris, for being you

Thank you, Len, for such liberal documentation

Thank you, Norman, for hours of checking and photo-copying

and

Thank you, June Gollifer, for disrupting your household and spending many, many hours at the typewriter.

Without these dear people there would be no book.

May God continue to speak through Len's ministry for many years to come.

PAT WRAIGHT

FOREWORD
BY BROTHER ANDREW

Dear Len,

I hope my wife Corry does not read this letter. You see, she always tells me off for singing too loudly in meetings. My problem is that when I meet with the saints and we start singing, I become totally oblivious to everything around me, and all I want to do is to 'make a joyful noise unto the Lord'. Since I am really no singer, my wife thinks it might disturb other people in the service—as it disturbs her. I wonder what the Lord thinks about that? Since you are now in a better position to know about that, I wonder if you can let me know one day.

Meantime, whenever I feel in the presence of the Lord, I want to sing my heart out and I don't really care what others think about it. I just love him too much to be influenced by others . . . well, kind of. . . .

That really makes me think of you, Len. You were heading one of the most dedicated and aggressive missions in the world, but somehow even there, your voice sounded different. Much louder, I would say, and a lot more impatient. It almost seemed to me you had a special 'hot line' to heaven, and it frustrated you that you were still singing a solo in the midst of all those who were singing with you. By the way: how is the singing going on today?

Just a few personal words, Len. I am so tremendously grateful to Iris for asking me to write a foreword to your biography. It meant I could read the manuscript long before the book was published and ever since I did, I have been preaching your sermons. Absolutely invaluable! What a wealth of teaching I found in it; impossible to resist the temptation to quote extensively from a book that had not yet been published. You don't mind, do you? You remind me in this so much of another favourite of mine, Abel (you probably know him), who through his faith is still speaking today: "By faith Abel offered to God a more acceptable sacrifice than Cain, through which he received approval as righteous; . . . he died, but through his faith he is still speaking" (Hebrews 11:4 RSV).

There's only one thing I remember where I could hardly believe you were serious. That's when you told me that on a door of a cabinet next to your bed, you had only two pictures. The reason: you wanted to see the two families in the pictures first thing in the morning when you woke up, so that you could pray for them. One of them was the Royal Family and the other was of Andrew, Corry and the children. I do not know which of the two families should feel more honoured, but I feel pretty sure that both needed your prayers very much. And I want to say a very big *thank you* for your prayers for my family, anyway. It certainly made *me* feel good, and I wish there were something good, really good, I could do for you so that everybody would want to read this book.

You remember, Len, all those young people who stood up to dedicate their lives to full-time service after we presented the claims of Christ to them? You will know more now about them than I do, but I pray and trust that many of them will continue in your footsteps—which is pretty hard to do: your steps were big. You climbed high, and you were rather impatient. But it all seemed right to me; chocolate soldiers don't do too well when the battle gets hot anyway.

Len, we were both far too busy to spend much time together, but one day I'll catch up with you and we'll have time to do what we couldn't afford to do down here. We'll do a lot of loud singing together for him who loved us.

Meanwhile, I'll keep in touch with Iris and the children. They seem very happy and they even 'smuggled' (that word is from the Irish) her into the big Mission 80 youth conference in Lausanne! How about that?

Now I really must stop, or I'll put people off—and I so want them to read the following fascinating pages that will lead them much closer to the Lord. At the end they will say, 'What a great God. He even used Len Moules, so there's hope for me.'

Thank you Len. Till we meet again and continue in his glorious service together,

Brother Andrew

CHAPTER ONE

GOD AT WORK

I had just passed my eighteenth birthday. Life in the factory had tested my religious faith and found it wanting. A flood of blasphemy, foul-mouthed workmen, filthy and suggestive talk poured their constant daily contribution into my young and fertile mind. I staggered before its impact, lost my footing, and was swept down its damning course.

In the swift current of those events my precarious position was aggravated by a young communist. Fluent in argument, convincing in manner, aggressive in his zeal, he ripped my spiritual faith to shreds.

'The Bible' he cried, 'is nothing but a tissue of lies and contradictions!'

Listing the names of great minds of agnostic thought who had forsaken the Bible, he finally challenged:

'No one in absolute honesty can look to such a book for guidance for life.'

My life was now a hell upon earth. Somewhere above the sun of faith and truth was shining, but I was in the blackest pit of unbelief. Like a swimmer being pounded by a succession of giant breakers crushing the very life out of him, I cried, 'Help!' and looked to God.

So writes Len Moules of his early days at work. (*Some Want it Tough,* CLC 1961, p.20).

Born in 1912, in Acton Green, London, the youngest of three children, Leonard Clifford John Moules was raised in a home that honoured God. His sister Gladys was already twelve and brother Percy ten when this younger brother arrived on the scene as 'an afterthought', as Len described himself.

As Len grew into his teens he became one of a group of young people at the Acton Railway Mission, with the girls round him 'like bees round a honey pot'. Among those girls was Iris Smith. Iris, heading for a dancing career, had very little time for the church; but she enjoyed the company of the other young people and was very attracted by the devastating young man in Scout uniform playing the organ.

A few years earlier an older couple had come from Cornwall and thrown their energy into working with the young people at the Acton Railway Mission. Godly people with a real love for young folk and a gift for communicating their faith, Mr and Mrs Bazeley brought a powerful challenge—and one by one the young people committed their lives to Jesus Christ in a very real way. Not only that, but they caught the vision of a single-minded commitment which set them apart to live for Jesus Christ alone. And they began to feel for people in other countries in a way which eventually drew many to leave home and travel to the far parts of the world as Christ's ambassadors.

Percy Moules, Len's older brother, was the first to step out and go to Bible School. Not long after completing his Bible training he set off for what was then the Belgian Congo. Len was fifteen at the time and not sure of his own direction in life, but seeing his brother set out meant a great deal to him.

I didn't know when we said goodbye to each other in 1927 we would never meet again on this earth. I am glad we did not know; it was painful enough to say goodbye as it was. Just a few brief moments together. I can feel his hand on my shoulder as he said: 'Len, I want you to be a good soldier of Jesus Christ. Read often 2 Timothy 2.' My eyes filled with tears as I stumbled away. In 1936 I sailed for India. As our ship passed down the Red Sea Percy was coming home on furlough up the Nile, so there were only a few miles between us. On June 2nd, 1943, he passed into glory, having laid down his life in the Belgian Congo. (*Some Want it Tough*, p.21).

A contemporary of Len's later said, 'One of the most influential things in Len's life was his godly father and mother. It was their faith which held him when as a young man he might have been tempted to slip away after the things of the world.' But it was touch and go.

Len was serving a five-year apprenticeship in electrical instrument making, and at the same time studying at night to earn his Ordinary National Certificate in electrical engineering. To quote Len's own words, 'Although I was respectable back at home and put up a façade of church life, at work I was foul-mouthed and pretty low-living, and life was empty for me at that time. It was then that I had a crisis.'

That crisis followed the cry from his heart for help when struggling in unbelief and attacked by his communist work-mate. God heard that sincere cry, and Len tells us how the answer came (in *Some Want it Tough*, p.23):

> How was it I never knew before that there was a sincere Christian workman near by? When I found him by the workbench I poured out my heart's miserable story. I told him of a tainted mind and of a breaking faith, of a discredited Bible

and of nowhere to turn. By his invitation I sat with him the next lunch hour and undid my packet of sandwiches while he took out his pocket Bible to read it together. A shadow fell across us and looking up I saw my Communist tormentor.

'You're surely not still reading that book, are you?' he asked amazed. 'It's full of contradictions and doubts, and— '

'Show me one, son,' my friend suggested, passing him the well-worn Bible. The young zealot fumbled the pages while mumbling that he had read the Bible many times. Then fighting to save his face, he said he would return the next day at lunch hour to discuss these points after he had had time to prepare. He handed back the Bible and was obviously glad to be gone. He never came back, and he never had anything more to say!

Returning one evening from night school at the Acton Technical College I realised I would always need Someone to help me fight my spiritual battles. Walking slowly along the lamplit street that showery night, I saw quite simply and clearly that the Christian life as God had planned it was that he should live in me. The price was letting him in, and letting him run my life. There and then I gave to God all that there was of me, and from that moment I was under entirely new management! The last two years of my apprenticeship were the beginning of knowing what it was like to be a victorious soldier of Jesus Christ.

Once the decision had been made to invite Jesus Christ into his life, Len turned away from the seamy side of things and sought to be a Christian example in every walk of his life.

It was during those early years after becoming a Christian that Len developed a great interest in the far-off land of Tibet. Mildred Cable and Doggett Learner, both with the China Inland Mission, caught his attention; he read everything they wrote about Tibet and their

14

work, and went to hear them speak when they were in London. Len was already convinced of his call to serve God, and now he became increasingly sure that he had a life work among the people of Tibet. As the conviction grew, Len took the next giant stride forward. In the autumn of 1933 Len left home to begin a two-year course at Emmanuel Bible College in Birkenhead, in the north of England. Speaking of his college days Len said,

It is hard to analyse oneself accurately, but I imagine as a young man I had a lot of Peter's personality about me. Impetuous and so often irresponsible. When the day came for me to enter a training college to prepare for overseas missionary service, I might have been my church's blue-eyed boy, but amongst twenty other men I was cut down to size — and very quickly at that.

There was another at the college who got my back up. It took all I had not to give him a broadside of my feelings. He was so slow, indecisive, with several other characteristics that rubbed me continually. I got through two terms by steering clear of him.

Arriving at the opening of the third term of my first year I looked at the accommodation list to find, to my horror, that I was to share a room with this paragon of provocation. I dared not ask for a switch. I just knew I had to accept it and all that came with it.

That night I saw in my colleague a different person. He was a man of prayer. He loved to read the Word. These two aspects of Christian discipline and devotion I seriously lacked. Within the week I was hungry to possess such a relationship with the Lord. To cut a longer story short let it be said that I was deeply enriched by his spiritual life. I needed him in my weakness. Because I needed him I wanted him. Because I wanted him all other previous repelling factors faded into insignificance. Bless God for putting me with this dear man that term (*Ascent of the Inner Everest*, CLC 1971, p.29).

15

While in Bible college Len had an experience which led to a deep resentment against the Roman Catholic Church, and this resentment festered within him for many years.

It was a regular part of the college syllabus to send teams of students out on trek each Easter. The young men set off on foot, pulling their equipment in a handcart, to preach in the streets and pubs in an area planned for them by the college staff.

On 4th April 1934 Len Moules and eight fellow students pulled their cart away from the college: destination Dublin! When they got there they immediately came up against opposition, and Len began to see a world very different from his own background in the Railway Mission at home in Acton. When they preached in the open air the night they arrived, hecklers demanded to know who had given them authority to preach and why they had no priest in charge. There was also argument over the authority of the Virgin Mary. However, this was a mere shadow of what lay ahead.

The night of 15th April was spent with a Mr Plunkett at Ballyroan Lodge, and the following day began on a light note. The entire team plus Mr Plunkett packed into a four-seater Morris car, having fixed the cart to the rear, and set off for a town twenty-two miles away.

Len describes an event which coloured his thinking for a great many years. 'Having dropped three of the team in the town,' he writes, 'the others went to make provision for the night. Returning an hour later we could see that there was a good open-air meeting going on. So we decided to hold a second meeting at the bottom end of the town. But before we could start the other fellows came to say they'd been stoned out of the square. At that one woman raised the jug she was carrying, saying, "If

16

you don't get out I'll smash your glasses off your face,'' and a hail of bricks followed her threat.'

Len continues, 'When they saw our text every one of the locals crossed himself and caused a great deal of disturbance. We had to pass through the square, but when we reached it we were greeted by a hail of stones which increased in intensity as we left the village. Things were looking serious. The crowd then began shouting and throwing boulders nearly the size of a man's head. One of the team stopped and asked for fair play, but a man stepped up to him and gave him a reeling blow on the cheek. As he was falling two of our chaps caught him, hurrying him away while two of us followed behind to ward off any boulders that might drop on his back. We were in desperate straits and took to running, trusting God for his protection. A mile out of the village they left us, although two followed on bicycles to be sure we were on our way.'

Len goes on to tell how they were not able to stay where they had planned for fear of reprisals and had to return to Ballyroan Lodge and their friend Mr Plunkett.

A further incident illustrates the strong opposition met by the team. One morning they spread round a small town and began to hand out leaflets from door to door. Len describes his reception as follows:

'I made for a few houses on the right of the main Dublin road. As I approached the door, two women came out.

'"Will you kindly accept this tract?" I asked, handing a tract to one of them.

'She looked at it, and turning to her friend said, "Here, Lil, you look at it." Lil looked at the tract, Lil looked at me and then, with the blood rushing to her face and her eyes staring at me, she tore the tract into pieces, her

17

companion applauding her action!'

So began a very real struggle deep in Len. Here were people who called themselves Christians and yet had reacted so violently against a group of young men also known to be Christians.

For many years Len was in conflict over this issue, and it was not until 1975 that the wound in his spirit was finally healed. Then Len and his wife were visiting the United States and staying with Dr Eddie Smith in Indiana. Dr Smith writes as follows: 'Len came to our home, accompanied by Iris. We occasionally met with a group of mainly Catholic charismatic Christians for a praise and prayer meeting, and we had been asked to take Len and Iris with us. As we left the house, Len said he didn't feel he should speak.

'However, the Lord had other plans, and Len was called upon to speak. By then Len had sensed the presence of the Lord and the love of the people there. There was a hushed silence, no one knowing what to expect. Len graciously stood up and, very hesitantly at first, gently told of the struggles he had gone through within himself over the years regarding Roman Catholics, and how God had broken down the barriers one by one. His final remark was that he believed this night the last barrier had fallen, and he asked forgiveness for the hurtful feelings he'd had towards Roman Catholics.

'What followed was a very moving experience— Catholics were praying and asking forgiveness for the wrong feelings they had towards Protestants, and Protestants were doing the same regarding Catholics.'

One of the Catholics who was present at the meeting describes the occasion from a Catholic point of view: 'This small Roman Catholic prayer community was usually uncomfortable when Protestant Christians came

18

to worship with them. So there was a certain tenseness in the group when Len Moules entered the room. We began to worship and praise God, but one could sense a holding back or heaviness as the time grew near for Len to speak. He began to share some of his experiences with Roman Catholics—the hurts, the fears, the misunderstandings; and as he spoke God's Holy Spirit moved on the hearts of those present. The very presence of Jesus entered the room sending a light into the dark corners of our memories and healing the bitter resentments that had been collected and nurtured over the years. There was a new freedom and unity within the community and no one could doubt that our Lord had performed a miracle of healing and forgiveness. Through the ministry of Len Moules we all now walk a little closer to God and to one another.'

The Easter trek of 1935 was undertaken on bicycles and covered 370 miles through Cheshire, Derbyshire, Lancashire and Staffordshire. This time Len was appointed trek leader. Two days before the trek ended the team visited St Helen's Junction near Macclesfield. Len writes, 'The people in this place put us to shame. Every night at 7.30 p.m.—prayer! Every morning at 6.30 a.m. —prayer! No wonder the Lord is blessing.'

From the very beginning of his Christian life Len was challenged by the need for prayer. He comments in his trek diary, 'We really believe that the success and the results of this trek are due to the morning times of prayer.'

Over forty years later and only ten weeks before his life's journey ended Len again spoke very clearly on the matter of prayer—this time to a young man setting out for the Far East for his first term as a missionary. At that valedictory service, Len said with characteristic honesty,

'As I look back I want to share something of what is on my heart and what the differences would be if I were a missionary again.

'I would pick up a verse in Zechariah 4:6, "Then he said to me, 'This is the word of the Lord to Zerubbabel: Not by might, nor by power, but by my Spirit, says the Lord of hosts.'" And as I look back over those twenty years in the north of India, tucked away in the Himalayas on the Tibet and Nepal border, I say that if I were a missionary again I would seek the Lord for a new life of prayer. You say, that's nothing unusual, is it? No doubt we all put that as a main priority. Yes, we do, but although we admit it, how does it work out in our Christian life? I have in my study a card which says, "Prayer Changes Things," and every one of you would say "Amen" to that. I could also say, "More things are wrought by prayer than this world dreams of," and you would all say "Amen" to that. I could say, "The devil trembles when he sees the weakest saint upon his knees," and you would all say, "Amen" to that. And one could add sayings and couplets about prayer which bring out this tremendous truth, and you would say "Amen" to them all. But although we all agree that prayer is no doubt the greatest dynamic of the Christian life, why is it, dear ones, that we spend less time on our knees than in doing anything else?'

At the end of his time in college Len began to make approaches to missions in order to find God's plan for his future. He first made enquiries at the China Inland Mission, but they only accepted workers for China. Anyone who had a desire to work in Tibet would have to go to China and see how the way opened from there. One man even patted Len on the shoulder and told him to go home and forget the idea of work with Tibetans.

But Len was not to be put off. Eventually Norman Grubb, who had stepped into the shoes of C.T. Studd, the founder of the Worldwide Evangelization Crusade (WEC), interviewed him and helped him with plenty of sound advice. On the basis of this vital contact Len sent in to WEC his application to become one of their workers. Part of his application read, 'I seek, by the grace of God, to be as balanced as possible in connection with Christian principles and my expression of the same. But I strongly feel the necessity, and thus urge as I am led, for the entire consecration of Christians that they receive a heart purified by faith and filled with the Holy Ghost. I feel that without such an experience no Christian can be a positive unit in God's service to overcome the powers of the evil one and extend the heavenly kingdom, or even help to bring back the King.' Strong words for a young man of twenty-three—and words which were more a vision than a reality until many years later. Looking back over his life, Len said in his sermon to the young man going out as a new missionary,

'There is another thing, too, that would be different. At the end of Matthew 28 it reads, "And Jesus came and said to them, 'All authority in heaven and on earth has been given to me. Go therefore and make disciples of all nations, baptizing them in the name of the Father and of the Son and of the Holy Spirit, teaching them to observe all that I have commanded you; and lo, I am with you always, to the close of the age.'"

'No doubt every missionary who has preached on this verse has divided it into four. Jesus said, "All power to all nations to teach all things and Jesus is with you always." The four "alls". But if we look at that verse we see that Jesus says, "All authority in heaven and on earth has been given to me." Couple that with the end,

"And I am with you always." If my arithmetic is right it means that in my life of discipleship when I am in the will of God and in obedience to his will, I have One who is not only with me, but One who is in me who has all authority. And as I look back on the years of my missionary career, I ask myself did I know all authority of the Lord Jesus Christ in all the situations which challenged me?

'Let me give you an example. It happened to one of the lady missionaries who was on our field, and I identify myself with her. It was in a Hindu village, and in that village was a woman who was demon-possessed. The Brahmins and other religious authorities of that village had done everything they could to try and get this dear woman delivered from demonic possession. It was an embarrassment to the village, an embarrassment to this woman, and also a matter of danger to all concerned. They had invoked gods and goddesses, they had done everything. They had left the spiritual realm and sought medical help in Almora, the nearest city. But the woman remained in this challenging situation. Until one day one of the elders of the village said,

'"We have a missionary living near here, and this missionary states that her God, whom she calls Jesus, delivered the demon-possessed when he was on earth. And she claims that this name of Jesus is relevant and has authority today. As we have exhausted all attempts and resources to see this woman delivered, may we not go and see if this missionary is able to help us?"

'The missionary was called and asked to come to the village in order to accept this challenge and see the deliverance of the woman. This missionary shared the story with us almost in tears. She arrived in the village a day or so before she was due to meet the village elders and, by accident, she was walking along a narrow path between houses when she was confronted with the demon-possessed woman. Before they got near to each other the demon-possessed woman stopped, and pointing to her said, "Ha! ha! ha! ha! What do you think you can do? You haven't got peace in your own heart. Ha! ha! ha!" And she turned, laughing, and went away.

'The missionary knew in her heart of hearts that she was impotent in this situation. She went back and dropped beside her bed, put her head in her hands and sobbed. Powerless! When challenged by the demonic kingdom she had no authority.

'Yet we read this promise from Jesus. I heard the passage of scripture concluded with, "This is the word of God." And I heard a response from you. Do you believe that all authority is with you? If such a situation confronted you, would that authority be operative?

'And I share it with you that at that time, I was just the same as that lady missionary. I would have had to put my head in my hands and sob, "Powerless! Powerless!"

'But I can humbly say that by the grace of God and by the coming of the Holy Spirit since that time, I know a little—I wish I knew more—of that authority.'

When Len sent in his application to WEC he made a request to God, and that request was answered in full. He asked that he should be granted 'a tough assignment' —no flowery bed of ease for him! God took him up on this.

And what of Iris Smith, who had been 'turned off' when Len was 'turned on' by his commitment to Jesus Christ? Asked whether she followed Len 'like a donkey following a carrot', Iris replied, 'Well, I've been a pretty persistent donkey. I have one friend who always called Len 'The Carrot'. But I had a crisis as well while Len was in Bible college.' Iris came to a personal relationship

23

with Jesus Christ in 1934, and a personal relationship with Len Moules in July 1935 when they became engaged to be married.

But more training lay ahead. Len's heart's desire was to reach the people of Tibet, but WEC had no work among them and planned to send this eager young man to the northern part of India to work among the Outcastes. This change of destination almost broke his engagement with Iris, who believed firmly that her call was to Tibetans. But Len, spiritually wise even in his youth, persuaded his bride-to-be that nothing could stop God fulfilling his purpose. If God had really called them to Tibetan work, he would so order their ways that they would fulfil his commission in his time.

With this in mind Len prepared himself as thoroughly as possible for the day when he believed he would be trekking high into the Himalayan mountains and meeting the Tibetan traders as they crossed the passes. This would mean weeks of dangerous travel, and sometimes months of isolation from fellow workers and modern civilization. In order to prepare for this, and because Len was interested in both the physical and the spiritual well-being of those among whom he would work, he obtained a place in the course held by the Missionary School of Medicine. 'What a grand year! One of the happiest and hardest I have ever spent. Work there was in plenty. Study—hours of it! But because of the interest and the contribution it made to our equipment for the future we took it in our stride. The more serious times of anatomy, physiology, and hard work were offset by the humour and fun during our free time.'

The course covered as many aspects of medicine as could be fitted into nine months. The students attended clinics with the doctors, casualty at Moorfields Eye

Hospital, and midwifery in South London. They had a hilarious time among themselves. 'Len was a great favourite with the doctors,' Dr Q. Muriel Adams remembers. 'He was full of enthusiasm and would go in on Saturdays to take a keen interest in the operations in the theatre. And he would be there again on Sunday to sing to the patients in the wards.'

The male students particularly enjoyed the dentistry, and in later years Len was filmed enthusiastically extracting teeth from a reluctant Tibetan! The students were also allowed to do a lot of minor surgery. The reward for this cram course was a diploma which was recognized and thought very highly of in missionary circles. However, Len comments, 'At the end of our training we were given some forms to sign. It appeared that our time at the Missionary School of Medicine had taught us sufficient to be dangerous men and women. We were obliged to sign that we would not practise medicine in Great Britain!'

Later that year, on 30th November 1936, Len and Iris walked on Acton Common, facing a separation of unknown length. They had much to share and were so absorbed in their last hours together that they were oblivious of a great event that caught the attention of thousands. As they walked and talked, blind to everything around them, the sky was lit by flames as Crystal Palace burned to the ground.

The next day Len was to sail for India. He counted it a joy and privilege to live by the motto C. T. Studd had handed down to WEC: 'If Jesus Christ be God and died for me, then no sacrifice can be too great for me to make for him.'

The date was 1st December 1936, and Len was twenty-four. His companion was a Canadian, Gordon Lewis.

An hour before leaving by train Len said farewell to Iris and his parents in the house in Acton that had been home. Len would not see it again for eleven years. 'Dad was about to commit me to God's care and keeping. Tears coursed down his cheeks as he brokenly asked God to keep and protect and use me. As I left the house, it came to me that God had taken all Mum and Dad had to give.'

Eric Gosden, a close friend from those early days, says, 'The time came when, settled in his own faith, Len's parents loosed him for God's service. They held him to their faith and they loosed him for God's service.'

CHAPTER TWO

NEW CLIMATE, NEW CULTURE, NEW CHARACTER?

As the boat from Marseilles bore them steadily eastward, Len and Gordon sought to prepare themselves for what lay ahead. Len wrote in his log of the voyage, 'The days have gone by swiftly and we have been engrossed in our language study with the help of two fine fellows who are Indians. I expect by the time we land at Madras a good grounding in the Hindi alphabet will have been attained.'

Later he writes, 'At last, on 21st December, the rattle of the anchor chain woke us up, and on looking out of the porthole we could see in the dim morning light the Indian coast and its lighthouse still flashing over the town of Pondicherry. This port of call has not a single motor boat, even for the police or governor. It has not even barges or lighters for the cargo, but all was done by the aid of dozens of curious craft called "chelingues". These are composed of the bark of palm trees literally sewn together, making the shape of a walnut shell. Each of these craft managed to bring to the ship about eight bales of cargo, and so all day they plied from shore to ship manned by the untouchables of India.

'It was our first sight of those with whom we shall be

27

working in the future. One woman on the boat remarked with a touch of sarcasm, "There are your future flock. They look happy, don't they?" Their unhappiness was conspicuous by the way they fought each other to get their craft near to the liner; it was seen in the huddled homes they came from on the shore; and I suppose it was seen in the single small coin they received after pulling those heavy craft many times to the ship.

'I did not see any sign of happiness in any face. The woman continued to say that they were used to it! Is that any excuse for them to remain in their sad benighted condition? Will such words satisfy the King of kings when he enquires whether his last command was carried out? Because we are used to sin in our land it gives no excuse for its continuance in the lives of millions.'

At last Len was able to write, 'It is Christmas Eve and we are standing looking onto the quay at Madras, at a group of Indians. As we came ashore the honour was conferred upon us of the placing of garlands round our necks. It was a real joy to shake hands with our Indian brothers, some from the untouchable villages around. What a change from the scene of Pondicherry! Here was happiness in reality.

'It was not long before I stood in front of the Governor of Police on board the liner to have my passport checked. He, on seeing the mission on which I had come to India, looked up with a smile and remarked on the greatness of the work, adding how young I was to start such a life in India. His assistant too, echoed his remark. And when standing at Customs, the first remark after the necessary questions regarding my outfit was, "You are young to start such a work here, aren't you?" I replied to all that to have one's life in front of you is the greatest help and privilege. Praise God for allowing me the honour of

28

stepping ashore in India at the age of twenty-four years.

'All through the night we travelled on to Benares, the most ancient city in the world. Our first view was looking down the river over its many stairs leading to the waters in which thousands were bathing, believing that their sins were forever cleansed, yet having no assurance of such a fact. For that assurance is only given by the Holy Spirit of God.

'You can guess how we scanned the scenery along the way as we drew nearer to the border and our station, noticing the monkeys, elephants, dogs and bullock wagons. We watched the fertile fields being irrigated by medieval methods, but more than all we looked ahead, for in the mist it was possible to see the peaks of the great mountain range of Nepal and the Himalayas.

'Stepping onto the platform at Nautanwa, we were greeted by the Indian Christian who was doing tract distribution on the platform. Not long after that we gripped the hands of other Christians who gave us a great welcome to the work at Nautanwa.

'The village is about 1500 in population, its inhabitants being Muslims, Hindus and Nepalis. In the few days we have been here we have been shown round the town, into the Outcaste quarters, through the bazaar, the dispensary, and so on.

'And now, as we settle in with the great mountains stretching along the border and reaching into the skies, and their great peaks gleaming with eternal snows under the rays of the Indian sun, we seek by God's help and strength to uplift his cross by life and lip, toiling at present in language study, that the men and women of India and Nepal may be numbered among God's own people.'

The weeks spent at the medical dispensary in Nautanwa were weeks of learning in every dimension.

29

It was necessary to give many hours to language study, but also to begin to learn the culture and customs of the Indian people. The field leader, Dr Wilfred Morris, was instructor to these young men. Len spent as much time as possible in increasing his medical knowledge and surgical skill by watching and assisting 'Doc'.

Len tells us, 'It was not long before the day came when we were sitting round the table, four of us, in the light from the pressure lamp. The map was on the table and Doc had spoken long about the future prospects.

'"Well, there it is," he said, giving the Tilley lamp a few pumps that shot up the illumination of the room and made the lamp roar, "We have the responsibility of this work away there in the North Almora District on the Tibetan border."'

So God *had* called Len to Tibetan work, and God had now opened the way for Len to obey his call. The Methodist Mission had been at work along the Tibetan border but now wished to withdraw from the area. They had sent a request to Doc Morris asking if WEC could take over the work. When Len heard this he felt 'as Abraham must have felt when God gave Isaac back to him'.

This was to be the beginning of the work to which God had called this young man from London, the work he was so eager to tackle and into which he was prepared to throw all his energy and enthusiasm. Certainly God had heard his prayer and given him a tough assignment. The people he longed to reach, the Tibetan tradesmen or Bhotya as they were called, trekked over the high passes of the Himalayan mountain ranges. To reach them it was necessary to meet them on the trade routes and in the villages many days' journey from the home base at Lohaghat.

A timid heart would have faltered at the thought of

30

crossing the vast mountain ranges on foot, but to Len this was a challenge. If the mountains were there and had to be crossed in order to share God's love with needy people, then Len would become a mountaineer and learn all he could about mountains. In his essentially practical outlook on life, he always made obstacles his special interest and challenge.

So Leonard Moules and Gordon Lewis travelled some three hundred miles east and north to the railhead at Tanakpur, and from there on by foot for a further fifty miles to Lohaghat. And this was only the doorway to the vast area of jagged mountains, deep valleys and roaring torrents they were to come to know and love.

Of course language study was a priority, but in those early months Len and Gordon pored over the map and estimated the supplies they would need for a long trek into the mountains. At last they set out for the Tibetan border on Friday, 24th September 1937. 'The trek took three weeks and a day. We covered a distance of two hundred and seventy miles entirely on foot, as the pony was a load pony.'

With characteristic thoroughness Len wrote a detailed log of each day, and from it we can gain a picture of the interest, hardship and excitement of that first venture.

'The mountains towered over the valley, at the bottom of which we could see the turbulent water of the Surja river and a suspension bridge made to look like a toy by the distance. Far below we saw the road winding to and fro, but we turned aside on to a little path that dropped fast to the bottom. These paths are made by hillmen and are direct from one road's bend to the other. They are called "pug dandies". By this we knocked some miles or so off the route and some fat off our bodies.'

One of the goals of this long trek was Mansiari village

where in 1912, the year Len Moules was born, a Miss Turner of the London Missionary Society had struggled against ill health to keep the Bhot Mission open. Under constant strain from the solitary life and the lack of funds for her support, this courageous woman left the area in 1913 and it had not been possible to find a replacement for her.

By the time Len was in his final year at Bible college in 1935, the London Missionary Society had handed over the work in that area to the Methodist Episcopal Mission. It was then carried out sporadically by local pastors and evangelists until the mission building was damaged by earthquake, weather and pilferage. The work again changed hands in 1936 when Dr Wilfred Morris, 'Doc' of Nautanwa, assumed responsibility on behalf of WEC for the area, called the Johar Bhot in the Pithoragah Tahsil.

Now, at last, Len and Gordon reached the area on a survey trek to assess the possibility of resuming outreach in Mansiari and other villages in the area. At one stage of their journey Len and Gordon were vividly reminded of the possible cost of working in those parts.

'One day we both went out to visit the grave of Dr Martha Sheldon, a woman who laid down her life for the Tibetans and Bhotyas. She died of the deficiency disease beriberi. As I stood by the grave of this woman who had loved her people with such devotion and Christ-like love, knowing God had called me to a similar task, I felt as if I were entering in on her labour. I could do nothing else in the silence of that rugged mountain slope but reconsecrate my life to God for these people. Praise him for being on the threshold of such work at the age of twenty-five.'

When speaking on the cost of discipleship thirty-five years later, Len shared with his listeners some of the things he had learned.

'Jesus says, "Follow me," and as an ambassador of the Lord Jesus Christ who has followed him for many years, I believe I have the authority to tell you what it means to follow Jesus.

'I would say this, as you move out in obedience to him:

'I cannot promise you a home,

'I cannot promise marriage,

'I cannot promise you children,

'I cannot promise you health,

'I cannot promise you the best of medical care,

'I cannot promise you security,

'I cannot even promise you a scar-less life.

'But I can tell you this. I can tell you that the promises of God are fulfilled in the generosity and the love of God. What he promises at every level is fulfilled to the dotting of the "i" and the crossing of the "t". There may be insecurity without, but there's security within. There may be fear all round, but there's faith within. I can promise you that you will find life, abundant life, a God-glorifying life and eternal life.'

Right from the outset Len proved the faithfulness of God. On the last Sunday of that long trek, the day after his rededication, he writes, 'We went to Sunday School at Dharchula on Sunday morning to find about thirty Christians gathered. These Christians were from Tibet, Bhot, Nepal and India, all living in perfect harmony and fellowship. I learned the golden text, Jude 21, in Hindustani and much to their surprise and pleasure, repeated it with the others: "Keep yourself in the love of God." Then I was requested to speak at the evening service and accepted. I spoke from Jeremiah 17:9, "The heart is deceitful above all things, and desperately wicked: who can know it?"

33

'After a little introduction in Hindi I spoke the message in English, and it was interpreted by the Rev. E. Steiner. I did not feel my vocabulary was full enough for such an attempt and did not want the minds of the people to be influenced and distracted by quaint and bad Hindi. At the close an invitation was given and about six came to the front. Two long-standing Christians wished to seek the Lord anew, and a Tibetan girl was received into church fellowship. Two others were the worst rogues of the district, whose lives could not be put down in print, and it was great to hear their prayers of repentance, after which they were put on probation. Two Hindus took their stand for Christ and one had his "chutya" removed (the lock of hair from the crown of the head, which is the sign of a Hindu and by which they believe they are caught up to heaven). It is a big test for them, and it was with great joy that we witnessed the hair falling to the ground. The other had already taken his stand in this matter, for when asked whether he wished his "chutya" cut, he said at once brightly, "kath gya" (already cut). Praise God for this stand.'

Len tells us that as they continued their journey 'I had a wonderful time with the Lord as I walked along. I realized my youth and inexperience more than ever, yet his grace and strength were ever at hand for me to appropriate. I am trusting him to help and guide in the great task ahead of the evangelization of Johar Bhot and this Tibetan border.'

Len and Gordon eventually returned to their base full of praise that the Lord 'had his hand upon us in times of danger and difficulty, and when food was running short he always supplied.'

However, behind all the success and elation there was still the Peter personality. Len was self-opinionated and irresponsible at times, and this did not always make things easy for his companions. But our God sees the desire of the heart, and Len tells how God dealt with him over this aspect of his life.

'I believe that if I were a missionary again I would go back with a new personality. Yes, a new personality! But surely, you say, our personalities are never changed. Yes, there's something true about that. No doubt some of us are slow and whatever happens we'll always be slow. And no doubt some of us will always be late while some of us are always early and no doubt will always be early. But I look back to the first period of thirteen years in North India and to a conference at Christmas time.

'We had our conference about two weeks before Christmas. That lasted a week, and then we had a week of fellowship together over Christmas before everyone returned to their place of work. It was a tremendous time, and at that conference we discussed the placing of missionaries and their activities. We would consider the whole year because some of us were a thousand miles apart, and until the next Christmas our communication would be by letters only. And here we could talk things out and speak things out and pray things out.

'One morning the father of one of our missionaries, who was staying with us, asked me if I would go with him for an early walk. I thought he wanted to see the dawn on the Himalayan snows. So I took him to a certain point and said, "That's the first peak that really gets the sun." He said, "I haven't come to see the dawn, I've come to chat with you."

'And I had an anxious feeling down in my stomach that he had something serious to say. He had. We sat down and he asked, "Len, do you know Galatians 2:20?" Thank God, I did; and I began to recite it:

I have been crucified with Christ; it is no longer I who live, but Christ who lives in me; and the life I now live in the flesh I live by faith in the Son of God, who loved me and gave himself for me.

In fact I never completed it, because half-way through he stopped me and said, "Len, I know you can say it, but what do you know of it? I thank you, Len, for letting me be with you at this conference, to see you plan on the blackboard where you are going to put your missionaries. That was not Spirit planning, that was human efficiency in the use of your missionaries. It wasn't God-given.

"'Len, I've heard you praying. Oh, that I could say it was the Spirit at prayer, but it wasn't. It was you praying with all your human desires, asking God's blessing on it.

"'You have fun at the table. If only I could feel it was Christ rejoicing in your midst, but not from you, Len. You are such a human human, Len, you know nothing of this. Oh, I know that you'd be willing to give your body to be burned, but Len, it is just in the energy of the flesh and you're asking God to bless it. You know nothing of this verse of Scripture."

'And he left me.

'It wasn't long after, possibly an hour later, that dawn came on the peaks, but that didn't exist as far as I was concerned. I was face to face with God on this issue. Thirteen years as a missionary—and if those works had been tested by fire no doubt they would have gone up as wood, hay and stubble. Human plans, human initiative, human ideas—good ideas. What I thought was best, sacrifice and what not, but was it the Lord's will? Was it spiritual decision? I doubt it. I know it wasn't. An hour later I lay down on the grass on that mountainside and spread my arms wide and said,

36

"'Lord, I am crucified with you. Oh, I live. Thank God for strength and a mind and a heart and a will and emotions and love. Thank you, Lord. I live, but not I, but you live through me.''

'And I went back to learn a new life. To seek the Spirit's will. To know the Spirit's touch in prayer. To allow the Spirit to live, so that it would be not I, but Christ who lived in me.

'If I were a missionary again, I'd want to go back with .a new personality.'

But back to the time when Len was still a newly-arrived missionary. 'In the last days of October the whole of our party moved down from Lohaghat to Lucknow for further language study,' writes Len in a prayer letter headed 'Crusade to the Outcastes,' the name by which Len's work was known in the early days. Having passed his language exam Len was sent down to Nautanwa.

'Thus I feel my vital work for the Lord has begun. I am here alone, living in the Indian house we came to twelve months ago. At the end of the mud veranda is the dispensary which opens daily at two o'clock.

'Each morning I have strapped my accordion on my back and set out with tracts and gospels and medicine for the villages dotted around. The accordion is still pulling the crowds from their homes to cluster round and listen to the glorious gospel message.'

Never short of ideas, Len tells us, 'At midday, hurrying to the station, I meet the train loaded with Nepalese as they flood through on their way to the border. I have put a trunk strap on to a tea tray, so as to hang it round my neck and thus sell the gospels more efficiently. I look much like a W. H. Smith's paper boy, I guess, and on my first day with this new paraphernalia a fellow rushed up and poured out a stream of Urdu at me. I did not know

37

whether he wanted a gospel, a tract, or two bars of nut milk chocolate! But daily some sixty free distributions are being given out and about forty or fifty gospels are sold each week.'

Len finishes his letter, 'My future plans are as follows. At the beginning of March I expect to leave Nautanwa for Bhot and thus the Tibetan border work will begin.'

And so it came about that Len, with great eagerness, set off to face what turned out to be a time of much testing. Looking back many years later, he said of that experience: 'Where I was working was twelve days' march very very deep into the Himalayan Mountains. The nearest white man was five days away and I was on my own for periods of up to four months. And I confess that on that camp bed, almost every day for nearly two months I sobbed and wept because of separation from family at home and Iris at home and my own missionary fellowship about ten days away. It was tremendous loneliness but I'm glad I went through it. God was with me during those days but they were days of deep trial for me, particularly the loneliness.'

Many years later, following his retirement from WEC Len moved into another sphere of work in a local church. It was there that his experience and the authority of the Lord Jesus in him were used to counsel others and to bring them to liberty and joy in their own faith. The testing and loneliness were a training ground so that Len could get alongside others and help them many years later. As a normal young man away from his colleagues, away from his fiancée and, no doubt, very much aware that he had a long time to wait for Iris while both Doc and Gordon were preparing for their own marriages, his problems were very real. A close colleague, the Rev. James Graham, shares that 'he had trouble with his sexuality as a young man, and I heard him counselling not only young fellows but even older men very openly about it. And how he used to pray and discipline himself and try to use spiritual methods, which he never despised. But he decided that this wasn't getting the job done and so he used to keep a mountaineering book or magazine by his bedside. Then if there was any pressure on him at that level, he would turn on the light and get absorbed in something that interested him and captivated his mind and took him to the mountains. The mountains were a tremendous challenge to him.

'The reason I mention that problem is that I was always impressed by the man's utter honesty. Many a man of his position and standing would have hesitated to talk about his sexuality, but Len didn't. It was part of him. Part of the common experience of being a human being. Where there was someone with whom he could identify, he would say,

'"Yes, I know what you are talking about. I know exactly what you are saying. Now here's the way I tackled it." He saw it very much like a groove in the mind: "It's rather like a groove on a gramophone record and the needle is prone to plomp into that groove because it's deeper. So what you have to do is fill up the groove and fill up the groove until you get it levelled off. Not destroyed, because it's part of our human nature. That's the way I did it. I filled up the wrong parts with things that interested me."

'Of course, what he was saying was that it's an act of the will. The moment we begin to exercise our will, the will of God comes in to strengthen us in righteousness, in the way God wants us to go. That's the way he tackled it and his counselling would be, "Yes, of course, all the resources of God are available, but maybe there are some practical steps you need to be taking along that line. Here's something I did.'"

Although the three years held times of acute isolation from friends, they were also filled to the brim with interest and new experiences. During this time Len's course in medicine proved to be invaluable.

'During those days in April 1938 my broken-down home had become the mecca of the sick and suffering. They came from villages far and near. Into mouths I popped pills and into arms I shot needles. Salts and aspirin wrought the most outstanding miracles.' Len, at twenty-six years of age, was the sole source of medical help. He pulled teeth, stitched wounds, eased pain, treated constipation and the opposite condition, and even operated on eyes.

So the work continued. While long black shadows cast their sinister silhouette over Europe and the world, Len filled every waking moment with outreach and medical care, treks to previously unknown valleys and to the yearly fairs or mela held in various villages.

One mela, held in Jouljibi, was a great meeting-place and therefore presented a challenge and opportunity to Len and others working in the area. 'It was the first day of the mela and the crowds were pouring in to make up the 15,000 that were present. Tents were pitched to make streets and shops and everything from rugs and blankets to horses and dogs was for sale. Values varied from a farthing to a hundred pounds and the purchasers came from Nepal, Tibet, India and the local hill country. The languages at the mela were Urdu, Hindi, Hindustani, Tibetan,Nepali, Pehari and Bhotya, all different.

'Those of us who went to preach the gospel were equally varied, coming from Tibet, Nepal, India, and America, and myself from England.

'There was a fine natural pulpit in the form of a huge boulder at the confluence of two rivers where the mela was held. We drew the crowd by playing a good marching hymn tune on my accordion and then took it in turns to speak in our different languages to the five hundred or so who had gathered to listen. It was thrilling as many pressed forward afterwards to buy a gospel.'

Meanwhile Iris, having also experienced the reality of God's love, went to Bible college and, at last, followed Len out to India. Len describes their brief meeting: 'I'm off on Saturday to meet my fiancée after three-and-a-half years apart. It will be a short two-day visit, and then up to the Tibetan border for permanent residence. When I shall see white men again I do not know, so pray for us. Loneliness has a price physically, spiritually and morally if one does not watch constantly. It is not till civilization is met again that the way one has slipped during the days alone comes as a shock. Personal care and appearance is the first step down, and soon the spiritual life is affected.'

Meanwhile the war was increasing in momentum. France had fallen and missionaries had to be called up. Len travelled to Bangalore and enlisted on 21st August 1940. He was in training until sent to Lucknow the following February. Wedding plans were going ahead, but not always smoothly.

'Everything was ready except my dress,' Iris tells. 'I had gone out with a dress which my sister had made, and I lost the whole trunk when I arrived in India.' Then Len tells of an unexpected complication: 'Suddenly I was mobilized to go to the Middle East. I had to wire Iris that all the wedding plans were cancelled, and to come immediately.'

Iris set off with a cake and yards of material while Len

applied for, and was granted, a special licence. 'We went to the minister on a Sunday afternoon and filled in a lot of forms. But it was not until we went to the church ceremony on the Tuesday that we realized we had already been legally married for two days!'

Having been mobilized Len was not supposed to leave the army base, but the colonel in charge was generous and sent the newly-married couple to Bombay to buy the equipment for the unit. So, as a brief honeymoon, Len and Iris negotiated for all the military needs of the 10th Indian Division of Queen Victoria's Own Madras Sappers and Miners.

The wedding day was 15th April 1941. By 28th April Len was away in Iraq—the first stop in five years of further separation, except for one leave after four years.

When Iris was asked if she considered that the long separations were worthwhile, she replied, 'It was worth every bit of it now that I look back. At times it seemed tough, but from the time we committed our lives to God and sensed the real purpose of life we kept to our motto, "Each for the other and both for God." Because we were both for God and that was our emphasis, he gave us a deep love for each other and a deep love for him as well. And through that love we loved other people and sought to let his purposes come through our lives.'

CHAPTER THREE

KEPT FOR TIBET

With Len involved in the Syrian and Iraqi campaigns, Iris 'made the three-day trip to our hill station, Abbott Mount. The mountain air was great after the heat of the plains. Before tackling the last three miles' stiff climb we stopped for rest and refreshment with Jessie Pearson and Ursula Burrows, two fellow workers who were living in the valley. On leaving I was suddenly kicked in the stomach by my mule, and before I could collect my senses the mule's back hooves struck a second time, hard enough to lift me off my feet. After a short rest I regained my composure sufficiently to mount and complete the journey, but had to rest for the next month. Doc Morris gave the verdict that it was a miracle I had escaped serious injury, and that I had been wonderfully preserved by God.'

A few short months after this incident God also wonderfully preserved Len, now an army captain, out in the desert in North Africa.

Len wrote to Iris, 'I must tell you of my trip through the German lines, running the gauntlet for about 120 miles. It was a great shock to realize that we were completely surrounded by the "Jerry", and it meant that about

12,000 men had to slip through their lines by some means or other. One advantage was that it was a completely moonlit night, which gave us a bit of a chance. I left with my small unit in my charge at about 9 p.m. and slipped out to join the larger group of about 100 vehicles at a rendezvous about three miles south. We then waited until it was dark and considered making a breakthrough, although we guessed that not many of us would see success. As it became really dark the demolition of Matruh started, and the Sappers just blew the place sky high. The ammunition dump shook the country for miles around, and a dull-red fiery glow spread until it lit the very heavens—a literal hell on earth. This demolition obviously told the "Jerry" we were out and on the task of breaking his lines, and so Very light after Very light went up, making the district around like daylight. It didn't need anyone to tell us that we were surrounded because we could hardly see two flares that were a mile apart.

'I felt rotten because I overheard two senior officers say that it was a 99·9% chance of being captured, and 0·1% chance of getting through. We waited one hour and it was the worst hour I have ever spent, knowing you were pretty sure to be a widow before an hour was up, or that I'd be shot in trying to get through. I imagined what wounds would feel like, or what it would be like to be blown up by a mine. I was scared stiff and in a funk. After about half an hour I realized that I was going to pieces and told myself that this wouldn't do. I knew that God had a plan for my life. I prayed that if the game was over and this was the final whistle, that I would go praising him and trusting him to fulfil the desires I had for Tibet. I strolled about trying to calm the Indian drivers who were mistaking the demolitions five miles off for an air raid, and I was able to sound cheery to one or two. I went aside

44

and prayed, "O Lord, I beseech thee for the sake of Tibet. For Tibet get me through this hell—fit and able to walk and climb for thee, not maimed, and for thy glory!" I repeated this time and again and qualified it, desiring his will. I was then quite calm and ready to die or live.

'We moved off towards the German lines, up over the escarpment. I had the first vehicle of the left-hand column. Some miles out I saw a vehicle which was obviously German, so I swerved to the right to miss it. To my astonishment three men came out with their hands above their heads. Driving with my left hand I drew my revolver, intending to make them prisoners, when to my surprise the first chap said, 'Golly! it's an Englishman." Here were three South Africans: a bombardier, a captain and a major. The first two were badly wounded, with shells still in the fleshy skin at the shoulder; the major was okay. Just as I was picking them up a "Jerry" tank came out of the mist firing at us; we just flung the chaps on the truck, and I let in the clutch and was away like the wind. After travelling over ninety miles through the German lines and camps, I knew we should be near our own positions. This made me careless in navigation and I ran into the Germans again in a big dispersed camp. The sentry spotted me and looked suspicious, so we waved to him and called out cheerily. But he was having none of it, and raised his machine gun. I drove to get a tent between us and then whipped round sharply, coming on him suddenly. He thought I was going to run him down and that put him off his stroke, and we flashed by at a good 40 m.p.h.. The bullets flashed by, some tracer, others exploded with a crack and weren't at all nice. Others went past a little slower. I did not stop to argue and just tore over the desert for half an hour doing about 30 m.p.h. all the time. Then we stopped to estimate our position.

'I was not in agreement with the major when he said the German lines were behind us, and the next camp I saw I tore through at 50 m.p.h.. Then the major shouted that the vehicles were ours. I knew "Jerry" had 80% of our stuff so I said, "Tell me another, I'm not stopping," and tore on. Then he spotted some Indians and yelled, "There's Indians here." This made me look round, and I saw Indians. Then I knew we were through, so I drove to the officer in charge and asked who they were; he told me and we gripped hands. The wounded went to the medical officer and I took the major for a cup of tea. We recounted the whole story and as we told it we both became more amazed. I declared that there was divine guidance and care over us. The major agreed.'

Len finished his letter, 'I have got the bullets which went into the tyre and truck. This has been a great strain, but even so I thank God I have come through still grinning, because I know I have been brought through by him for Tibet. As I look back and see the inferno of fire I am amazed at the numbers of men that are getting back. Some have brought their guns and other equipment in, others have walked in with only their clothes to their name. I am the only officer of five in our unit to return, and only three Sappers made it out of twenty-nine. We are still hoping they will come in or that we may re-capture them as we push the Germans back.'

Len's story was reported in full in several newspapers, including the *Dundee Evening Telegraph* and the *Exmouth Journal*. As he writes of his escape it sounds exciting, but there were very dark times for Len and countless others during those years. For instance, the stench of decaying corpses in the heat of the desert was so appalling that Len took to smoking a pipe for a time when helping with the burials.

Following the eradication of almost the entire unit under his command, Len was sent to Larnaca in Cyprus to remake and train a new unit. He attended the Crusader Church of King Richard in Larnaca and organized and led a choir during the eleven-and-a-half months he was stationed there.

Then came a return to the front and service right up Italy until at last, on 9th March 1945, he landed in Bombay en route for 61 days of well-earned leave.

But the call to the Tibetans had not been in any way dimmed by Len's war experiences: 'Iris and I, as day by day we looked Tibetwards, felt our joy would be full if we could meet our Bhotya friends. The trip to Mansiari would take two weeks of hard, exhausting travel and rob me of of the rest for which I was sent on leave. Then came the news of the Thal mela only five days' journey north, a round trip of one hundred and twenty miles. We both felt it was our God-given opportunity.

'On the ninth of April, towards evening, we set off down the road to a government rest house about five miles away in order to cross the hot river gorge early next morning and climb the six miles out the other side before the sun could cook us. Then we were on our way.

'A visit to the Methodist Mission at Pithoragah cost me a lecture to the students in the high school on my experiences in Libya and Italy. At the next village an old friend of mine, the Mussulman community grocer, greeted Iris and me and gave us a great welcome. Everyone wanted to hear about the war.

'The fourth day brought us to the mela. Looking down from the mountain, the shingle beaches of the river were covered with ant-like figures moving from booth to booth, purchasing wares from the Bhotyas. People were flocking in from every road and path. What a riot of colour!

We followed the road down the hillside and across the river, passing the stone temple throbbing with folk at their varied duties.

'On the far side was a group of shops, and it was there that we hoped to find our Tibetan trader friends. Sure enough, they were there just as I had left them some five years before, seated on the stone wall spinning their wool and talking together. They recognized us at once, and I doubt if there was another spot in the whole world where so many grins were on view at one time. Then the tongues began to wag, and my trips and tours of the intervening years were explained and questions answered. When was I coming back? That was the burning question and the most difficult to answer. But that we were coming back was definite, and to prove it we put in hand a contract for repairs to the mission house at Mansiari. That night we lay on our beds tired, but so happy.

'The homeward trip gave opportunity for further calls on old friends. Although it was an exhausting trip physically, it was a great spiritual boost and victory for our souls. We both praise God for the event.'

The war was not yet over and Len had to return to his military duties. But 'God again gave of his goodness by bringing about an India posting, and thus not allowing me to return again to the front'. This was a double blessing as Iris was by now expecting their first child; Noel was born on 29th December 1945 at Bangalore.

Despite the joy of being with Iris and of Noel's arrival the nine months at Bangalore were hard; Len was obliged to hear the court cases of men who had betrayed their countries while serving in the forces. Most of these men had served in the horrors of the Burma front. Len rarely referred to his task, except to share with Iris that his life was threatened as a result of this unpleasant duty.

Nine months later, on 16th February 1946 at Bangalore, Len was released from the army. Dorothy Gruber, a fellow missionary, tells of Len's return. 'The long wait was finally over and Len came home. He was different to what I had pictured. I had heard about his happy-go-lucky, mischievous ways but he was more sober and very, very weary. It was a kind of weariness that doesn't go away quickly. Shortly after he returned Doc Morris handed over the field leadership to Len and Jack Cairns, and Doc and Nancy went on a long-delayed furlough.

'During Len's period of leadership I had more to do with him. I found him very easy to talk to and very understanding. He was getting rested up now and a bit more lively and full of fun. When Doc and Nancy returned from furlough it wasn't long before Len, at Norman Grubb's request, formed a separate field called the Himalayan Border Field. It was clear that the Lord had given Len leadership qualities, no doubt helped by his stay in the army.'

Commenting on their years of separation, Iris wrote home, 'In closing I would leave you some words of Miss Amy Carmichael: "the hallmark of a true missionary is refusal to be weakened or soured or hardened or made hopeless by disappointment." As we stand together in the fight, that hallmark shall be upon each of us for his glory.'

'As the train thunders north, mile upon mile is being put between us and our military station,' writes Len in a letter dated 14th April 1946. And he could have added that a long and gruelling chapter in his life had come to an end. But Len's eyes were on the future. Although physically exhausted, spiritually he was exuberant and filled with enthusiasm at the thought of picking up the threads of his work on the Tibetan border after a break of five long years in military service.

'We halted en route at Fatehpur in the United Provinces, where we spent time with Doc and Mrs Morris who were about to leave for England on furlough. From there we pressed on to our new headquarters, opened as a base for the Tibetan work. At 6,000 feet up and forty miles from the railhead the headquarters acts not only as a home for the missionaries working in the area, but also as a store for medicines, tracts, gospels, tinned food for emergency supplies, stationery, and so on.'

With military precision, Len began to plan his strategy to reach as many as possible with the gospel. 'The end of April will see the mountain track slipping under my feet as I move to the border again. Iris and Noel will be remaining at the headquarters. What my eyes will meet on arrival at Mansiari I don't know, as the mission building collapsed during an earthquake on 4th June last year. Already my preparations are being made—a rucksack lies in the corner of the room; jersey, sweaters, fur helmet, ice axe are in another corner; medical equipment, tracts and gospels are packed near by.'

Years later Len spoke of those early years with regret. 'Now that I can look back over twenty years of evangelism in India I just wish a young man in his twenties could have the head on him of a man of sixty. He would certainly do things differently. But the Lord is good to us; in those early days we made many mistakes, but the Lord taught us. As the years have gone by things have become emphasized which I'd love to have known and had as priorities in those early days.

'I remember the day when I put up on the wall an inch-to-the-mile map of the Himalayas and prayed that there would be a pin in every village. And I walked my knees almost to the ground, carrying a pack with gospels and preaching. A pin went in, another pin went in, two pins went in, and soon the map was covered. I remember being somewhat despondent after a few years at the results we had seen. Friends, yes. People whose homes were open, yes. But those who were giving their hearts to the Lord Jesus Christ, so few. And then I read in my Bible about prayer and fasting. That's it, that's it, I thought. It's not just getting around, it's prayer and fasting. So the pendulum swung. I remember a long period of fasting, and a long period of prayer. Even the mail from Britain wasn't opened for a number of days. I fasted from food and everything was for God—because I thought this was the key.

'This had been going on for some time and then a little voice inside said, ''Why are you on your knees here praying and fasting while souls are dying out in the villages?'' So we went back to the villages and back to putting pins in the map.

'The pendulum swung from prayer and fasting to evangelism and trekking. Well, which are the priorities and what has the Lord taught us?

'I'm not saying these things are wrong. I'm just telling you how the Lord dealt with me and, no doubt, how the evil one got me swinging and unsettled in the commission God had given me.'

As it turned out, this first long trek after Len's demob was anything but the triumphant return to the work he had planned. Everything was against him. He tells us in a long report in *World Conquest* news magazine for September 1946:

The devil met the preliminary plans for this survey trip for future work with a winding blow when we heard of the earthquake that had demolished the Mission building in Mansiari.

51

I confess we had to shake our heads and get our wind back. When we penetrate the heart of the greatest mountain range in the world to have our 'Camp 1' wiped out like this it has a big influence on the work and success of the missionary.

But this blow was offset to a large degree by the willingness of Jonathan Lindell to accompany me on the trip. Our applications to two government departments for permits to travel in this area were therefore submitted. Almost at once my permit arrived and plans went ahead. But three weeks before we were due to set off the second blow fell when Jonathan's permit was refused and no reason given. We began to realise the evil one was going to resist the work on the border of Central Asia in no uncertain manner.

I felt I had no choice but to go it alone accompanied by a Sherpa porter named Kinjuk Tsering, a Buddhist by religion, whom Jonathan sent over to take his place.

Then came another disappointment. We were to leave on Monday morning and the previous Saturday a young lad came to the door. He was the owner of the pony which we had hired to carry stores and other goods. He was sorry but he was unable to come. He was afraid to venture into the far off districts where the men were rough and came from Tibet!

This brought us to rock bottom but we decided our last hope was for me to carry my kit and bedding weighing 52 lbs. and Kinjuk the food and utensils weighing 80 lbs.

We set off and climbed to 7,000 feet and I must confess my 52 lbs. very soon seemed more like 500 lbs. Then in six miles we dropped to 4,000 feet where a Rest House was balm for an aching body and sore feet.

My diary reads, 'May 7th. Woke at 4.0 a.m. and hit the road by 5.0 a.m.' We had twenty-one miles ahead of us that day and seventeen miles were steadily uphill.'

So day after gruelling day passed.

We were six days out and only two to do, but there were still two high passes to cross. I was about beaten and felt I could carry my load no further. I managed to get a local to carry it for that day's journey.

At last we reached Mansiari and were standing in the Mission compound. What a sight! Rubble and timber all in a mad heap. Roofing slates and purlins stuck out from the heap in total desolation. I felt a lump in my throat and was not far from tears as I turned away to look for some place where we could live.'

This was not the end of their troubles either.

It seems that for two long months it had rained day and night. The crops in the terraced mountain fields lay sodden. The food for the journeys to the Tibetan markets lay rotting in the fields. There was a famine ahead. I had never seen the grim spectre of famine as I did then. Men, women and children all bearing the haggard and desperate look of those who face the most awful of deaths—famine.

Day after day the rain poured down. Heavy mists rolled up from the valley below to condense on the snowy peaks and fall in rain. The temperature dropped, and one morning on looking out we saw that the hills and passes were covered with new snow. And still it rained.

I had intended to go further but none of the porters approached would take money to cross the 17,000 foot passes. They would do it if paid in food and then decided that even for food they would go only as far as the foot of the pass.

What a black prospect. We had food for only two months at our rate of consumption—these men would eat three times our quota a day.

We could not wait. There was no food to be had. And then news came that the rivers were now raging torrents. The crude timber bridges spanning the waters were in danger of being swept away. This would leave me isolated for more than four months with insufficient food and too little equipment to be of any medical help.

Thus the odds against me mounted up and there was nothing I could do but pull out and return to base.

Before leaving I opened a small crate of gospels and gave

one to everyone coming to the compound who could read. Also, during the last few days, I visited several villages to see folk too sick to move and was able then to distribute gospels and witness to them.

The road back has to be seen to be realised and understood. At one point the path was several hundreds of feet sheer above the river. The path was just three feet wide and slippery with the sodden manure of many animals. With our heavy back loads a slip could have had only one result. But, praise God, he kept his word that, 'he will not suffer your foot to be moved.'

The rest of the story of our retreat is best left unwritten. Let me just say that I eventually fell off a hired horse outside the Mission headquarters with blistered feet and septic legs having taken a thorough beating. It was a month or more before I was really fit again, but even before that we were planning our return.

In a letter sent home to England Len writes, 'After a few weeks when my legs and feet had been healed, Andrew Laing and I pored over a map of the area around our HQ. Of the 2,500 square miles of mountainous country, much has remained untouched since our arrival here ten years ago. Beaded pins stuck in the map gave us a quick account of the work expended and what yet remained.'

That map and its pins almost became an obsession. Years later Len again refers to the map when talking about the need for prayer. 'There was something else which cut into my prayer time and that was a huge map on the wall, an inch to the mile. Every village was marked on it. And some of the villages had a red pin put in which meant they had been visited. Some were 14,000 feet above sea level, some 3,000 feet above sea level. Some five miles away, some ten, a long day's trip there and back again. But a pin had gone in because the gospel had been preached there and as a young missionary I wanted to see red pins in every village on that map. As soon as my prayer time was finished, the knapsack filled, and the few that had come to the dispensary had been given medicine, I was away! And tired at night after limping in with a blister, the first thing I did after I'd taken my pack off was to take out another pin and in it went—another village with the gospel. I longed for the day when that map bristled like a porcupine, when there wasn't a village that hadn't had the gospel. That's what I lived for. I knew hunger and I knew thirst. I knew what it was to carry the pack in the heat of the day. I knew what it was to crunch over ice. I knew what it was to be walking along the road to another village when the temperature was 115°F., bringing the gospel, witnessing, witnessing, witnessing.

'Yes, I was willing for all things. But if I could go back I don't think there would be that map; in fact I know there wouldn't be. You see, I read in Mark 1:35, "And in the morning, a great while before day, Jesus rose and went out to a lonely place, and there he prayed."

'In Mark 6:46 it says, "After he had taken leave of them, he went up on the mountain to pray."

'And in Luke 5:15, "The report went abroad concerning him; and great multitudes gathered to hear and to be healed of their infirmities. But"—what is this I read? They were coming to you, Lord, to hear the gospel and to be healed but it says, "he withdrew to the wilderness and prayed."

'Lord, did you leave those who came to hear? Did you leave those, Lord, who were there in the crowd and were ill? In fact I remember, Lord, reading previously that you sent the crowd away. And no doubt when you sent them away there were things said about you. I can almost hear them; "You won't heal me because I'm a Samaritan."

'But, Lord, I understand now that you had a priority, you withdrew—for prayer.

'Lord, when I look back on my missionary career and those twenty years, I believe I got things in the wrong proportion. I was long on witnessing. I was long on sacrifice. But I was short on prayer. And I've come to realize, dear Lord, as I look on your relationship to the Father, that your authority and power was proportionate to the time you spent with the Father. No doubt you would have been powerful in my ministry—there would have been power, Lord, in that expression of your life in me and through me, if I had spent more time with you. It could be that I would have left behind the very incarnation of Jesus Christ in a few more. Perhaps they themselves would have been blazing this precious gospel in a language that was their own, in a culture in which they'd been brought up, in an understanding of their own nationality so much more effective and better than that of this foreigner no matter how much he loved them, who wanted to get a red pin in every village.'

Such maturity came after a lifetime of experience, but back in the early years there was great dedication, boundless enthusiasm and a deep caring for those under his guidance.

The following February Len and Andrew Laing made a trek to the Nepal border lasting two weeks, and from 10th March to 10th April 1947 a Tibetan survey was made in Sikkim. As Len said, 'Witnessing, witnessing, witnessing.'

But the big one, the return to Mansiari and beyond, was planned for May to July of 1947 before Len and Iris returned home for furlough after eleven years away from England.

This was to be the survey trek for future advance. Among the piles of equipment were a cine camera and enough film to make a record that would challenge those who saw it at least to pray—if not to hear God's call to leave home and trust God as part of the Tibetan border team.

Len wrote about this trek at length in his book *Three Miles High*, the name he gave to the film of the trek. He wrote of it again in even greater detail in his autobiography, *Some Want It Tough*.

It was an epic affair with Len accompanied by Jac Dyck, a Canadian normally responsible for WEC work in Nepal. But this time the weather was hot, the flies in great evidence, and lice so abundant that Len and Jac early on bravely shaved each other's heads and continued as bald as a couple of eggs! The intrepid missionaries climbed with their hobnailed boots, their khaki shorts, their shaven heads—and to crown all, Jac carried a rolled umbrella.

On their arrival at Mansiari they found that the desolation of the mission building was accentuated by a covering of tall stinging nettles. Jac shook his head and declared it beyond repair, but 'late that night the light of a hurricane lamp revealed two kneeling figures praying that God would enable us to make the necessary survey. This would establish the coming reinforcement on the borderland of Tibet and enable Christ, the light of the world, to shine in these villages.'

That year, 1947, it was possible to go beyond Mansiari. So, after giving medical attention to many over the next ten days and sharing the gospel with all who came, Len and Jac pressed on through one of the greatest gorges of the world to Milam. As they were going north the traders loaded with merchandise and accompanied by sheep in their hundreds were coming south. Others, having disposed of their wares, were returning north. In the middle of all this, often on the narrow mountain footpaths, were Len and Jac with their drovers and pack animals.

Beyond Milam they were climbing, climbing, up and up, until the danger was from frostbite and the ordeal was to find the physical strength to reach the summit of the 17,000 foot pass. Then it was down the other side with the track obliterated by three feet of snow and deep drifts waiting to engulf anyone taking a wrong step.

To make matters worse, the drovers became snow-blinded and were unable to advise on the route. But, as Len said in his account of the trek, 'we had not had one accident or a moment's illness during this whole period, and were deeply grateful to God for his gracious provision and journeying mercies day by day.'

CHAPTER FOUR

TIMES OF CHANGE

It was on 8th September 1947 that S.S. *Strathmore* steamed up the Channel, bringing Len home after eleven years' absence. With him was Iris, returning as wife and mother. Noel was twenty-one months old and another member of the family was expected around Christmas time. But if anyone had the idea that Len was coming home for a rest, they were certainly mistaken.

This burning enthusiast, now thirty-five years old and with his tremendous experience of the war and of the mountains to which God had called him, never considered rest as part of his curriculum. He had matured and mellowed, but his zest for life was as great as ever. His furlough was, in his opinion, a means to an end.

Hadn't he and his companions surveyed the Himalayan peaks to research the possibility of a much greater work among the Bhotyan people? Hadn't he shot reel after reel of film of those arduous treks over the top of the world? Furlough was to be the opportunity he needed to tell as many as would listen about his work and the need for more to join the ranks of those committed to reaching such isolated places with the gospel.

Of course, furlough was also a time to get together

with families at home and to renew and strengthen friendships. But it turned out that Iris was the one to spend time with the families, while Len fulfilled an incredibly heavy schedule of meetings for showing his film and sharing his vision.

The autumn of 1947 was spent largely in preparing the film and splicing it together. There were a few meetings, such as the WEC Annual Rally, at which Len was given an opportunity to speak. Then Carol, the first daughter, was born on 1 December, and Christmas was spent with Len's parents before the flood of engagements burst upon him. The film, entitled *Three Miles High,* was ready for use, Len was raring to be off, and Iris laughingly remarked that she 'saw even less of Len than when he was off trekking in India'.

There are records of ninety-three meetings through that year, scattered far and wide over England, and this number does not take into account a visit to Ireland and a programme of some length in Scotland. There were camps and conferences and school assemblies. The majority of the great number who came saw the film while others saw Len in the robe of a Tibetan lama, wearing his hat and his shoes and with his prayer wheel in his hand.

Len reports on this whirl of activity, 'News will have travelled to many by now of the great blessing accompanying the tour with the film. A new aspect of deputation work has arisen—we wonder, not how many are coming, but will we get them all in? We are interested in about forty men and twenty women who have voluntarily asked us about the work.'

It was during that year that Len was privileged to be interviewed on the radio programme *In Town Tonight,* and was also granted the honour of an F.R.G.S. for his work done in the Himalayas.

As the end of 1948 approached, news of *Three Miles High* spread further afield; the entire month of November was spent in Scandinavia with Phil Booth and John Lewis of WEC as Len's companions.

Throughout the year at home Len had been working on a script for his film, writing and rewriting it so that the film could be used once the family was back in India. But Len continued to show the film himself until the very end of his furlough on 24th February 1949. The voyage was a long one and Len was ready for conference back in the Himalayan HQ by 27th March.

Back 'on the job' in North India, Len's duties took on a different slant from when he had first arrived over twelve years earlier. Then he had been the enthusiastic new boy fresh from England and eager to get on with the task God had given him. Now he returned as field leader, with the same enthusiasm but with considerable responsibility to carry. Then he and Gordon Lewis had begun to assess the possibilities before them. Now the team had increased to seven and plans were made to place personnel permanently at strategic places in the mountain villages.

To begin this new phase of the work Len called a conference of the team, which took place from 27th March to 4th April 1949. A letter home written in April gives a taste of the excitement that must have accompanied this thrust out of team members: 'The last week has seen the station abustle. Jessie and Kay (Jessie Pearson back from furlough, and Kathleen Leslie who joined the team in 1946) have been packing and sorting out tracts and medicines for their permanent move over to the Chamoli district, where they hope to establish a base for the work among the Niti and Mana Bhotyas and Tibetans. In another room the three men (Percy Breusch and Dudley Barker, who came out from Australia in 1947, and Marlin Summers from the USA, new to the team in 1948) were writing down what they needed in order to be self-supporting for six months in the far-remote village of Milam. Milam is 12,000 feet above sea level, under the very brow of the Untadhura Pass into Tibet. Oh, it's just grand to see these remote valleys being permanently occupied. Vision is becoming fact.'

For Len a tremendous change had taken place. Before his furlough, if anyone went to these distant places he went. Now, as field leader, it was his job to see that others were equipped to travel many days from base and survive physically, mentally and spiritually. Len was one always challenged to pray, so included in the resolutions of the Spring Conference was a section headed, 'Prayer. It is requested that each Crusader spends one day a month in prayer, laying aside all duties to this end. It is suggested that stations set aside one meal each week for united prayer and fasting. The need for the above is obvious.'

At the same time Len was reading widely. In particular, he was reading his Bible with an understanding that was to bring blessing and encouragement to those far beyond his present sphere of work in the years to come. As a thoroughly practical man he was able to apply this gift in a unique way by taking the facts of day-to-day life and applying them to the truths he found in the Scriptures.

Some twenty-five years later Len still used illustrations from his days in the Himalayas to help put over Bible teaching. A favourite example of this is the story of Bachhi Ram's shop, which he used to bring out the truth of James 1:4.

The Authorized Version's rendering of this verse is,

'Let patience have her perfect work, that ye may be perfect and entire, wanting nothing,' but Len used the following amplification: 'Let patience have its perfect work, that you may be perfect and entire, and fully stocked for all who pass by.' He enlarges on this verse, 'no matter what the need may be, there is a spiritual resource that can meet that need.' To bring this point home he continues, 'on the Tibetan border we lived four or five days' journey deep in the Himalayas. There were no motor roads then; everything went up on the backs of coolies and on mules, ponies, and yaks. Where we lived there was a small Indian bazaar, and naturally in twenty years I got very friendly with some of the shopkeepers.

'There was one whose name was Bachhi Ram, and Bachhi Ram would wait for customers outside his shop. When you went in you saw oil lamps, you could smell spices. He had rugs, he had kerosene oil, I don't know what he didn't have. His was the all-purpose store. And Bachhi Ram would sit outside on an old, bent, metal chair. Or he would stand up, holding his stomach and looking out benignly on the world. One day I was passing through the bazaar and there was Bachhi Ram.

'"Salaam, Bachhi Ram," I said, in Hindi of course.

'"Well, Sahib, where are you going?" he asked.

'"I'm going to the Post Office."

'"What for?"

'"I have to order things up from the plains. Things you don't stock."

'"But, Sahib, what is it you want?"

'"Bachhi Ram, I want things you don't stock," I said.

'"Well, tell me what you want."

'"Bachhi Ram, I have a Corona typewriter," I told him. "I want a black-and-red Corona typewriter ribbon which you don't stock. I'll order it from the plains."

"'Sahib, wait a moment." He disappeared into the dark recesses of his shop and was gone about five minutes. Then he came out, puff-puffing to get the dust off something in his hand. "Is this what you want, Sahib?"

'There it was, a red-and-black Corona typewriter ribbon!

"'Thank you, Bachhi Ram. Yes, that is what I wanted. Salaam," I said as I paid and went back home.

'A week later, I broke the mantle on my Aladdin lamp. These were very hard to come by, so I thought I would put in an order down to Bombay for a dozen of these mantles. I went down, but as I was walking through the bazaar I was arrested by,

"'Salaam, Sahib," and there was Bachhi Ram. "Where are you going, Sahib?"

"'I'm going to the Post Office, Bachhi Ram."

"'What for, Sahib?"

"'Well, you don't have it, Bachhi Ram. I've got an Aladdin lamp."

"'Yes, I know you have an Aladdin lamp."

"'Well, I've broken the mantle and you don't stock them, and I'm going to order up some from Bombay."

"'Sahib, wait!" He went into the shop and he was gone quite a time. I thought, ah! he hasn't got any.

'Then he came out, blow puff, puff blow, at the dust, "Sahib, is this what you want?"

"'Uh—oh—a box of Aladdin mantles. All right, Bachhi Ram, thank you very much. Very good of you." And I went back.

'Some months passed and we had illness in the house and we needed sulphanilamide ointment, so I thought I would get the first post down and order some up from the plains.

64

'I had to pass Bachhi Ram's shop—there was no other way. And as I went past there he was watching.

'"Sahib. How are you?"

'"I'm very well, thank you."

'"Where are you going?"

'"I'm going to the Post Office."

'"What for?"

'"Look, Bachhi Ram, I want some sulphanilamide ointment and you don't have it. I've got a child that's sick and I need some from the plains and I'm ordering it up."

'"You want sulfananamide"—he couldn't even pronounce it—"You want sulfananamide ointment?"

'"Yes, that's what I want, sulphanilamide ointment."

'"Wait, Sahib." And he went into the shop. And this time he was gone nearly a quarter of an hour. I thought he'd forgotten all about me. I was just getting up to go down to the Post Office when he came out.

'Puff, blow! Blow, puff! "Sahib. Is this what you want?"

'Sulphanilamide ointment!

'"All right, Bachhi Ram, thank you very much."

'Now I was there twenty years and I don't want to give you the impression that he always had what I wanted. But the thing I never thought he'd stock—somewhere in the back of that shop, there it was. Oh, we had some fun. In fact, over the years it's been a bit of a competition as to whether he had everything I needed.

'I'll be honest; 80% of what I wanted, he had in that shop. How he got that stock list, don't ask me.

'But then I read this verse, "that you may be fully stocked for everyone who passes by." And I tell the Lord I want to be a spiritual Bachhi Ram's shop. Then, for example, when a young man comes along who has a need, he shares the need. And like Bachhi Ram I say, "wait a minute", and I ask the Lord to remind me what I have in stock. Into my mind come the experiences of perhaps 1935 or 1936 and the Lord urges me to share them. I can tell that young man what I went through and how I was helped. It meets his need, and after prayer together he goes away refreshed.

'And so it is that others come with varied needs. My prayer is that I might be a spiritual Bachhi Ram's shop, "fully stocked for all who come by."'

And yet, as wisdom and experience were gained, Len was the first to admit that in the early days he had executed his duties with the precision of a military campaign. With maps and charts and the little red pins, men and women were dispatched to this place or that with the very best intentions. As Len shared so often in later years, 'I had almost an army officer's concept about the whole thing. I said, what are the points for doing this, what are the points against doing this. Let's weigh them all up. And obviously there were more reasons why I should do this than why I should do that. So I decided to do it this way. They were human plans in human strength. I was asking God to get his divine pen out and initial it and say that he would bless it. I'd never come to him to ask him if this was the way he wanted it. Nor had I asked him for his strength to do it. I was a young man and I was at the full flood of a young man's strength. It was wood, hay, and stubble. And if it had been tested it would have gone up in flames.

'Thank God, my faith would have held, but there would have been nothing I could bring to the feet of Jesus. It was human ingenuity. Tremendous ideas. Good ideas, although I say it. I'd have thought God would have reached for his divine pen as fast as he could so I could get on with it.

66

'For thirteen years it went on like this. Thirteen years! When I think of it I get a cold cramp in my tummy. More than half the time I was out there gone, through this other personality of the flesh.'

Perhaps a little of this organizing ability shows in a letter home sharing the great news that permits were to be granted for a three-month trek into Tibet. The deep desire of Len's heart seemed about to be fulfilled.

'In between the administrative duties and much correspondence, not forgetting giving language lessons, I have tried to tackle the elementary stages of Tibetan. Why? Because we have been told that our application for three months' trekking in Tibet next year has been granted! This news came from Milam through the Tibetan trade agent. We await the official permit which is on its way via the government of India in Delhi. What a wonderful answer to prayer!

'Already a file here contains sheets of notes re stores, transport, tracts, equipment, medical stores, and route. It is going to take a good deal of prayer, thought, and time. Much of this must be settled by November when we make transport dates with the Bhotyas.'

Ken Booth shares another aspect of Len, 'Len had the ability to encourage new workers and also to make them feel that they were an integral part of the team. It was astounding to me that he should ask me to speak at and conduct the communion service for our field conference, which was held just two months after I'd reached the field.'

But there was one person Len evidently found it difficult to identify with at that time—his own son, Noel. Again it is Ken Booth who brings this to light. 'It was obvious to some of us in the early days that Len had difficulty in accepting his young son, Noel. Noel seemed to be the opposite to everything that Len desired in a son. This seemed to bring out a sort of rejection, some resentment, perhaps, towards Noel. Poor Noel was timid and very, very sensitive, not strong, and suffering quite a lot from ill health in various forms. On my arrival on the field this was an obvious area of Len's difficulty. I personally tried to involve myself in it and tried to encourage Noel to be bolder and more venturesome.

'It was a great joy to see Len with Noel numbers of years later, and to hear Len speak of Noel in glowing terms. Len had grown to love Noel and appreciate him, particularly as Noel learned to overcome the difficulties that he had faced. He showed to Len a type of young manhood which Len was very proud of.'

In April 1974 Len spoke with the love of a father for a son, and showed the respect in which he had come to hold Noel. 'My son is twenty-eight years of age, and he's in charge of the religious education of a school for 1,900 children in Sunderland. As we were walking together about a month ago, I was saying, "You know, Noel, the thrill of it is that we are walking in a day when God has given us the fullest recovery. We're back again in the New Testament church, Noel, and I'm excited at what God is going to do."

'When he had heard me out and I had dried up, he said, "Do you know, Dad, I'm not really interested in the New Testament church."

'"Oh?" I said.

'"No. And I'm not really interested in the recovery of the Holy Spirit."

'I looked at him. I thought my son had gone a little off the rails.

'"Look, Dad," he said. "That is how God expressed himself in those years to the church. What I want is not recovery, but discovery of the Holy Spirit in the age in which we live."

'While I digested that he continued, "Dad, you don't want a Corinthian church, do you? With incest and all the brawlings at the Lord's table and all the rest of it, do you?"

"'I think you're right, Noel. I don't want that," I said.

"'Well, that was part of the New Testament church. Surely, Dad, what you want to see is the Holy Spirit expressing himself in his fullness in the day in which we live? In our groups and churches; in our fellowship with each other; in the way which is relevant to the age in which we live?"

"'I'm with you, Noel," I agreed.

"'It's not the New Testament church we want, Dad. It's the church of the twentieth century. It's not the recovery of the Spirit but the discovery of the Spirit in the age in which we live."

'My son turned my eyes from looking back to looking forward, and I do believe that in these thrilling days in which we live God has given the fullest recovery of all we had lost.'

The 1950s were tremendous years for Len and Iris. It was go, go, go all the time for Len while Iris had a major role to play in bringing up their family and in making the base a real home for all who were there. Ken Booth's wife, Cecily, takes us into that home in her memories: 'One of the things that comes back so clearly is the evenings we used to spend round a great big roaring log fire. Iris used to buy in very cheaply a huge coolie basket full of oranges of the type that were easily peeled. These would be dumped down in the middle of the floor in front of the fire, and all of us would gather round. Some would be doing study, which very soon was abandoned, and we used to eat oranges and spit pips in the fire while Len would be in the forefront and talk and joke and laugh. I remember Len clearly for his joking and his teasing and his laughing.'

Cecily's father, Frank Martin, was the one used by God to bring the crisis in Len's life that changed his entire future. From the time of that visit, when Len was faced with the challenge of dying to self and allowing Christ to live in him, his natural efficiency came under new control.

Len said later, 'Looking back I can truly say that my fully committed life in Christ began at that time. I was satisfied at last.'

Others saw the change at once. Cecily Booth continues, 'I remember very vividly the good times we used to have in Abbott Mount. We used to gather together, I think it was once a week, for a prolonged time of prayer. I remember the singing and Len playing the piano and the tremendous times of fellowship. I remember Len's humility and his willingness to be touched by the Lord and to weep before the Lord. His sensitivity to the Spirit was so helpful to us. There was no evidence of leader and follower in that respect. We were just all in it together. That was one of the things about Len that came through so clearly.

'One occasion illustrates very clearly Len's humility and willingness to hear the voice of the Lord, and his softness of heart. Dudley Barker gave a message based on Paul's "what things were gain to me, those I counted loss for Christ". And the Lord touched us all very closely—there were very many things that each one of us sought afresh to lay before the Lord. But the first one to his feet when Dudley finished was Len. He went straight into his office with tears streaming down his face and back he came with all his certificates—certificates of the Royal Geographical Society and so on that he'd had framed and hung round his walls. And his medals too, and the whole lot were placed on the table as unto the Lord. And he said, "I don't care what you do with them. They no longer matter to me." They did eventually go back on his walls, but they ceased to have any pride of position or place for Len. It was so indicative of his humble walk before the Lord.'

Tears were no sign of weakness in Len. They were a sign of the new Len's humility to God. Ken Booth says, 'Len was a man's man, and had the ability to draw out and make the most of the human resources around him.

'His favourite mountaineers were Mallory and Irvine, not because they attempted to reach the summit of Everest from the north, but because of the spirit they showed. Len had a picture of them with the caption, "Last seen going strongly for the summit." Quickly aware of the various capabilities of his team, he asked me if I would paint this picture for him. I believe he kept it with him right to the end of his days. That was Len's attitude, too—"Last seen going strongly for the summit." He had the ability to inspire, and incidents like these are remembered now with the same challenge coming through.'

W. H. Murray, deputy leader of the 1951 Everest expedition, describes his meeting with Len in the foreword he wrote for Len's own book, *Some Want it Tough*:

In the year before setting out on the Everest Expedition of 1951, I went out to the Garhwal Himalaya with a small exploratory expedition. After much climbing on mountains near the Tibetan frontier, we cut eastwards through a great gorge named the Girthi. We could find no record of anyone having traversed it for sixty years past. We made that

71

crossing (twenty-two miles) in six days of hard work. Descending into the bleak and glaciated valley of the Goriganga, we at last arrived at the village of Milam. It lay on a broad spit of land between two rivers—nearly two hundred houses set among green fields. It had an open, sunny situation, for the great peaks were set well back.

We walked into the village, the farthest outpost of Indian civilisation, remarking the neatness of the houses and the cleanness of the courtyards. Every man, woman, and child looked healthy and well-clothed. As we passed through its narrow lanes, we were astounded to see a young Englishman coming to meet us. We had only to look at his face to realise that we had met a man with a purpose, and therefore of abounding vigour, disciplined by a keen sense of humour. His first words astonished me still more,

'Are you Murray?' he asked. Not only had he heard of our arrival in the Gori gorge last night, but had also traced our journey up the distant Dhauli gorge before we ever tried to penetrate the Girthi. The Milamwals (people of Milam) had long ears.

The more we came to know Moules and his Bhotyas, the more we came to like them. Like us, Moules was a mountaineer. Unlike us, he had chosen to sacrifice an outstanding physical ability to an ideal of service higher than ours. Had he chosen our course—who knows, he might have taken part in the attack on Everest. When I think of the huge sums of money spent upon that mountain and the human energies poured out, and then reflect upon the work done in the Himalaya by Moules, I cannot help but wish that men might spend with equal ardour on the inner Everest what is so lavishly devoted to the outer.

The mountaineers conquered Everest, but Len had a great disappointment. His deep desire had always been to enter Tibet, but he writes with feeling, 'I have to tell you of the failure to get the Tibetan permit, due to the official being absent from Gartok and far away in Lhasa.

This was a great blow to us. However, it is amazing how our own plans are often not what the Lord has for us, and his ways are better and higher than ours. This was proved again that same night when Dayan Singh, a secret believer, came to my house and offered to take the Tibetan Bibles into Tibet.

'A few days later the precious volumes were packed on the animals' backs, and I tramped to the top of the nearest ridge with Dayan Singh. We then had to part, and I admit that my eyes were misty and I was not far from tears. With a last handshake he began his trek to the passes and Tibet. The first pass, Untadhura, was 17,590 feet; then the Jainti, 18,500 feet; and lastly Kungribingri, 18,300 feet above sea level. Dropping down on to the rolling hills of Tibet he made his way towards Gyanima, five days' journey off. But after three days he came to a small market town of tents. Here Dayan Singh had the opportunity of giving out three Bibles: one to a government official from Lhasa, another to a high lama from Dunchyu Lamasery, and a third to a lama from Choringwo Lamasery.

'One day out from Gyanima, when the men had pitched tents and were cooking food, shots were fired from the rocks above the camp and all was confusion. The servants were unarmed and, on the second volley of firing from the bandits, fled into the hills. The robbers then came into the camp and stole fifteen mules loaded with bales of cloth. It so happened that the box of Bibles was wrapped in one of the bales of cloth. This news was received with mixed feelings, but it is good to know that Tibetans regard printed pages with great reverence and are loath to destroy them. They think ill will come to them if they destroy such things. Therefore we can be assured that those Bibles will be read and not destroyed.

Next year we are hoping to send in two yak loads of Bibles and New Testaments.'

However, big changes lay ahead. Len tells us 'how mainland China "liberated" Tibet and became responsible for foreign policy and internal defence'. He goes on, 'The Indian government has quite rightly tightened up on the border regulations and on security measures. We trust that time will prove that our work is solely spiritual and social and has no political interests whatsoever.'

So the years passed with increased loads and greater challenges. Tapes were made in the hill dialects and in Tibetan and Nepali and sent to Gospel Recordings to be made into records. The medical work continued. Len taught at the language school and Iris had women's groups for sewing and teaching. There were the other team members to care for when they were sick, and of course the children. There was finance and correspondence. And there was the occasional wedding to plan and make nearly as memorable as if it had been at home. Also there was the joy of building up and teaching those who believed, and a multitude of other commitments that grew with the passing years.

Phil Booth gives an insight into those growing commitments. 'In 1954 I met Len again. There weren't many things going on in the hills, or on the plains near the hills, that Len hadn't got his finger in. He was chairman of this and chairman of the other, on this particular committee and that particular committee. If anything moved in the Himalayas of an interdenominational character, Len was in it. He was on a school trust. He'd got his finger in the pie at the Mussouri bookshop, which eventually we organised into the CLC (Christian Literature Crusade), and it was amazing to see the

74

breadth of that man's ministry in that part of the world. And of course he had a tremendous rapport with the Indians themselves.'

Little by little the pressures bore in on all the workers, and at one point Len shared, 'It has been a hard year. Children's illnesses, pressure of work, discouraging reports from vital areas of recent blessing; all quietly made an impression. The stress and the strain did not remain only outside. To some came the thought that we might crack, but God raised up dear friends in prayer. His loving care for us in response to such prayer brought us through recently to a new release.'

One of these pressures was that the mission house in Mansiari, which by this time Len had helped to rebuild, became inaccessible to the team when the border was broadened to keep aliens away from the entries to Tibet. However, the sting was taken out of this disappointment because 'we prayed much about a national worker taking over this work and area beyond the Inner Line. God touched and challenged a young South Indian student, Mr A. K. George, who had just finished three years at the Yeotmal Seminary. He has already been up on a survey trip and was with us in conference when we were really united.'

And then unexpectedly, at a time when the pressures were considerable, the Australian WEC Headquarters invited Len to 'prayerfully consider a tour of Australia and New Zealand. The team here were unanimous that it was of the Lord and that Iris and the children should go with me! This meant a big step of faith, but we have planned and booked for us all to go.' Len then asks for prayer and continues, 'It is no easy thing to follow Norman Grubb, but if the Lord can get his message across through me, and Len Moules doesn't get in the

75

way too much, he will surely meet people and call them to himself and his service.'

On 2nd September 1954, Len and the family sailed for Australia.

CHAPTER FIVE

LIGHT AND DARK

As with all Len's major adventures of faith, every tiny detail of his first visit to Australia and New Zealand is recorded meticulously in his clear handwriting in a large hard-backed notebook. Every date is given, every meeting listed, the approximate number present tabulated and the numbers of those who responded to the message duly noted.

Leaving India as winter approached, Iris must have found a rest through the spring and summer of the Southern Hemisphere most welcome—as was the sunshine and good food for the children. But Len began a heavily-loaded whistle-stop tour that was filled to the brim with activity, from Perth to Adelaide to Victoria to Queensland to New South Wales. He was in Tasmania when Beth, the last member of the family, was born in the Queen Victoria Hospital, Melbourne, on 11th December.

Over the years Len was deeply concerned about how he could fulfil a busy schedule and at the same time be the kind of father he knew he should be. When talking of the children in one of his letters he admits that 'their parents seem to be always so busy. Please pray that we may be guided to keep the balance and not rob the little ones of the love and affection and time they should have from us.'

Of course this is easier said than done. They arrived in Australia to find the programme fixed and people eagerly expecting to see and hear 'Major Leonard Moules, F.R.G.S., WEC, Pioneer and Leader of the Tibetan Border', as he was generally billed.

As Len records, 'The six months' tour covered about thirty thousand miles, entailing three hundred or so meetings,' and that does not take into account a number of radio broadcasts. Len's engagements in Australia continued right over Christmas and into January 1955, when he flew to New Zealand to as heavy a programme over there. This lasted until mid-March, and then it was back to Australia for a final twenty-six meetings in eighteen days. They boarded the *Himalaya* for the voyage back to India tired, but eager to get back to the job awaiting them.

As it turned out, things never were quite the same again. No longer could Len trek up to Mansiari and open his clinic for his Bhotya friends. The dream of entering Tibet had ended with a rude awakening; not only was Tibet out of reach, but so were the great snow-covered passes, the five miles of steps, and many of the other places that had been a part of Len's life. 'The young man, Mr A. K. George as he is always called, had arrived in Mansiari and the bungalow, land and furnishings had been registered as a Christian trust for the continuation of the work. Ken Booth was the last of our men missionaries up in the north and he closed down the work. The Garhwal work on the border has also been closed down for a number of reasons and the lady workers have left with regrets at there being no one to carry on.'

Other sides of the work, however, were active and encouraging. 'The Landour Bible Institute, started two or three years ago, is a project whereby correspondence courses based on the word of God and Christian living, in English and several vernacular languages, have been sent out. Without any advertising, the students have grown from a mere half dozen to nearly three thousand in two years. Already three of the team are working full time on the project and they are now hard pressed to keep up. Our vision is to translate the courses into Tibetan and Nepali, with added staff to handle the work entailed.

'The Tibetan Gospel Hour continues night by night in its fifteen-minute broadcast. The radio is bringing a message to the areas which as yet have not been manned by a missionary in person.'

Cecily Booth comments about those times, 'During our second conference the subject of finances on the field came up and it turned out that Len was the treasurer as well as the field leader. As the money was received from various home bases he would send a full allowance to the outstations, regardless of the amount received, so that Iris was left to run the house with what remained. His attitude was totally self-sacrificing in this respect; he never looked for the money for himself.

'After I'd been ill that first year, Len graciously arranged for me to go to hospital. At the time I didn't realize what was involved. I was sent down for a check-up without any thought of how much this was going to cost. I was never once asked for the money—I realize now that I should have paid, but I didn't know at the time. Len's attitude was totally generous in this respect. He had another attitude that has been a blessing in many ways but was not always understood. He felt that the

Lord's servants deserved to have all that was needed in order to do the job to the very best of their ability. If he ever had occasion to go down to Delhi to see about visas he would stay in a top hotel and go around in taxis, which horrified some of the more parsimonious members of the fellowship. But he claimed, and rightly so, that he could get done in a short space of time double the amount of work that anybody else could do by hanging around in poorer situations and without transport. Len learned the hard way that it doesn't work for everybody. Len would go into a situation with his military-strategy type of mind, execute whatever he had to do with precision, order and speed, and get out again before he'd run up too much of a bill.

'Presuming that this was the right way for everybody, he sent one young couple down to chase up permits for Mansiari and gave them *carte blanche* to do the same sort of thing. They weren't quite able to achieve the same speed; they ran up a much bigger bill than Len ever did and billed it to the field. There was quite a bit of reaction on that occasion!'

Len was not one who found fulfilment in desk work, but he had a way of giving of himself in personal correspondence. He could challenge, enrich and encourage in the same way that his preaching and teaching were so helpful to each individual listener.

Ken Booth tells us, 'I had a lot to do with Len in the area of correspondence, in which medium he was able to come through with warmth and depth and relate to you as an individual. At one time I was alone in Mansiari and faced a crisis in my life, and I asked for permission to leave the work and return to Australia briefly. Len's correspondence carried a deep sense of identification, and yet a real challenge to my accepting the lordship of

Christ in my life. I could accept these things from Len because I knew my leader himself had experienced most of the things which he asked his team to handle. I found Len was always easy to approach. He was one to whom you could always open your heart, knowing there was a sympathetic ear, an understanding heart, and a wealth of wisdom to be gained. Encouragement was one of the key aspects of his life and ministry.'

Underneath the super-efficiency and military precision there was no hard-headed dictator, but a very sensitive and gentle-natured man. He told one friend, 'Never confront me with a crying woman; I just can't stand it,' and Ken Booth hints at this side of their field leader. 'One point that seemed to come through from time to time was Len's difficulty in confronting people with issues. Some of us thought that Len was a little weak with the ladies in particular, a little bit too tender-hearted, perhaps. He didn't want to have a showdown on an issue which a number of us felt needed to be taken up.'

But one of the single ladies, Hester Withey, shares how Len came across to the lady workers, 'Those of us on the field who were single were very much aware that Len and Iris had a particular understanding of the situation and problems of single people. They had both been single on the field for some time—longer than many, in fact. They had to wait so long before they could be married, and then after they were married they had that long separation while Len was in the army. Both Len and Iris had to put their own relationship on the cross so many times and in so many ways that it gave them a real understanding of other people. I'm sure that that's why the Lord allowed it. It made their leadership far richer and far more effective than it would have been otherwise, even though it was costly to them. We were aware that some of their badgering and joking back and forth together was a way of communication in the middle of community life, when really they could see one another privately very little. It was a way of having fellowship together in spite of all the crowds around, when they would probably have very much preferred to have had their own little home.

'Both Len and Iris always challenged us to the highest. Len was always committed to the highest in life; he challenged himself to discipline and hard work and not taking the easy road. At the same time, he had his little indulgences and he enjoyed fun and holiday and change. He wasn't an ascetic in that sense. But he worked hard and expected everybody else to work hard with no shirking. He was a real challenge in the physical realm, by example, in the Spirit and in word. His talking and preaching was a challenge to be free of self-indulgence, self-pity, and looking for the softer way. He challenged us to be willing to be tough for Jesus' sake and face the difficulties without being sorry for ourselves. All this was so good for the rest of us as we were coming along.

'Len was good at keeping confidences, and that makes a great difference for a leader too.'

But, to return to Ken Booth, 'Towards the end of his period in India, when Len was not involved himself in the actual field ministry but was more at the administrative level, we found that he was unable to say "no" to invitations regarding meetings, commitments and responsibility on various committees. As a result he became very tired and under pressure, and we as a team had to ask him to list for us his various obligations. Then we took it upon ourselves to cull it and cut out those responsibilities which we felt were not in line with his priorities. This probably seems a very strange thing for a team to do to a man who had such tremendous qualities, but he was very tender-hearted and found it almost impossible to say "no" to any demand.

'It was during this time that the team began to spread out into different areas, away from the familiar territory that had been Len's particular burden and vision. Len seemed then to be looking into other possibilities of ministry. At this time, I think, the question of his becoming Manager of Weinberg Allen School arose. The field actually had to step in as a responsible body and give its voice against such a move.'

These were some of the problems that faced a man who desired to be one hundred per cent available to God; he found himself drawn towards being over-available to the demands put before him. To give Ken Booth the last word, 'Looking back we can just thank the Lord for Len, and thank the Lord that Len made himself available for the Lord to manifest himself through him. Len was an outstanding leader; warm, vibrant, living, very human, intensely affectionate, very obviously fond of his wife. People, particularly his fellow workers, were his main asset and concern. He had a commanding presence with a distinguished bearing, and could take his place without effort in any level of society. He obviously loved the Lord and was whole-hearted in his expression of that love. We would just like to thank the Lord that we had such leadership in our early missionary endeavour. We believe that it was the Lord's preparation for the task we have had for a number of years.'

Len himself said about leadership, 'A leader must have the vision of his total team plus fifty per cent more.' When Ken Booth later took over the position of field leader from Len, Len advised him, "Ken, you're taking over a team of wild horses. Whatever you do, make sure you keep their heads all in the same direction. If they ever get tangled in the harness you've had it."

Ken felt that, 'to be asked to take over the leadership following Len was to be asked almost the impossible, for he had set such a high example.'

The handing over to Ken and Cecily Booth by Len and Iris was precipitated by the need to return home on furlough to place Noel and Carol in boarding school. This tremendous decision, which faces so many who are willing to step out in obedience to God, caused much heart-searching. Right through their young lives Noel and Carol had been in the whirl of community life with loving parents who had to respond to other demands. Now there was to be even less opportunity to be together as a family.

However, in the perfect planning of God, there was among the language students at this time a lady who had been a deaconess at Carey Baptist Church in Calcutta. Along with the rest of the team, she had benefited and been enriched by the breadth and depth of Len's Bible teaching. Somehow, alongside all his other activities, this amazing man had made time to dig deeply into God's word. He had studied to find the original meaning of words, he had read widely to bring Bible situations and characters alive, and he had given Bible instruction in morning prayers and also at the Kellogg Church in Landour. Len had taken a week of Bible readings on the subject of forgiveness at that church back in August 1953. The readings presented such a challenge that those attending requested that they should be put into print. Some copies are still read and valued.

The language student from the Calcutta church knew that the pastor and his wife, the Rev. and Mrs. Walter Corlett, were due to take leave and needed to find someone to take his place as minister of his church. Because of Len's close association with the Kellogg Memorial Church, he was asked to act as Pastor from July to September 1955. He deemed this an 'inestimable privilege' as it gave him the opportunity to bring 'a devotional ministry to over four hundred missionaries spending their short vacations in the cooler climate at Landour. To be able to accept this invitation to the pulpit where Carey ministered is the greatest honour Iris and I could have had given us.' As it turned out the invitation for three months extended to five, and Iris believes that those months were 'the cream of the twenty years' ministry in India'.

In April 1956 the missionary, ex-British Army major steamed up the Channel on a Polish ship flying the Red Flag! This was intended to be just another furlough, but God was soon to reveal that he had a very different plan.

The changes in the Himalayan situation, Len's many commitments, and his role as a Bible teacher brought Len and the family home in a state of uncertainty. They knew they were at a crossroads, but had no clear lead as to their future. Four years earlier Len had believed that the Lord was telling him he would return to England to take responsibilities there. With their love and under-standing of young people, both Len and Iris thought this could be at candidate level; Len had written to Norman Grubb, who was International Secretary at the time, but nothing came of it. Another WECcer, John Lewis, was Deputation Secretary and suggested that Len might use his speaking ability in that way. But here they were back in England with no clearly defined task ahead of them. Len had not put behind him the invitation to be Manager of Weinberg Allen School back in India, and perhaps this pulled him the hardest. The invitation still held, and as

Len and Iris had both been drawn to the offer they kept it before them as a possibility.

However, on their return family came first. Having spent a while with Len's parents, they all went down to Cornwall to Iris' sister and brother-in-law, Nancie and Willie Rodda, at Scorrier.

Throughout Len's life he put so much enthusiasm and zeal into all he did that he had periods of great weariness. At this stage he experienced a certain amount of depression. Jack Aitken, his friend and fellow worker both in India and England, shares that it was 'a dark depression when he felt at the end of himself, of no use, and that no one wanted him'. He was physically exhausted and God, in his perfect timing, met his need. Over the past years a Dr Fraser Kerr had been sending homoeopathic medicine out to India for a problem that troubled Iris. Dr Kerr was in Cornwall when Len and the family arrived, and he visited them for a day. The following morning he unexpectedly arrived back at Scorrier to say he was concerned about Len and was writing to the WEC headquarters to advise that Len should have a period of prolonged rest before taking up further duties.

Where better to rest than on a turkey farm and creamery? Where better to unwind than with loving relatives, his own family, round him, and nephews and nieces who always enjoyed his company? David Rodda, who was nine at the time, tells us, 'I always knew that Uncle Len cared and was interested in things.'

But Len, despite his weariness, was unable to spend these weeks in idleness. He and Willie Rodda devised a scheme which not only gave Len a challenge, but also opened a new branch to the creamery that still continues. They adapted an Austin A70 pick-up by raising the height and increasing the length—and Major Moules the missionary became Major Moules the cream salesman! Through the summer of 1956 Len set off with his brightly painted, loaded van, declaring, 'Cream Makers since 1890.' His job was to sell jars of cream in bulk to shops all along the coast from Newquay to Bournemouth, anywhere he could make a sale.

As Len rested and the depression left him, he began again to speak at meetings. The days of the cream round had been days of renewal and the therapy he needed. As ever God did more than that; the small payment Len received was sufficient to supply Noel and Carol with their school uniforms for their entry into boarding schools in September.

In October of that year, 1956, big changes lay ahead for WEC, and these were a pivot on which Len's own life swung in a totally new direction. One of the staff, Francis Rowbotham, sets the scene: 'The WEC staff were gathered at the British headquarters in London. We had a big decision to make; we were waiting on the Lord to know his will concerning the leadership of the mission in Britain. Norman Grubb, who was son-in-law to C. T. Studd the founder and pioneer of WEC, had been leader since the early days, and we realized the responsibility we had in choosing his successor. Len was at home on furlough from his work in India at the time and was with us at the staff conference. He was set on returning to India and was almost ready to return, but as we looked to God he made it clear to us that here was the man whom he had prepared for such a responsibility. Len was asked to be willing to seek God's will for him. Was it to be India again or leadership in Great Britain?'

It wasn't an easy decision, though difficulties were resolved and the appointment accepted. Writing of the new appointment in his final letter to prayer supporters of the work in India, Len says with feeling, 'It is not to be mentioned how totally inadequate we are for this position, and to follow folk of great maturity and stature in the Lord. But their God is our God and "He will never, never, never, never, never (literal translation) leave us or forsake us".

'Thus for us a chapter is closed, another begins. We must know God in spiritual altitudes now, not geographical. We would give our right arms to go back, but we know God's appointment for us and we must get our roots down.'

Many years later Len's successor, Robert Mackey, described Len as 'more airborne than chairborne', and the change that came to Len's life-style through the appointment as British Secretary was a difficult transition for this active man with such a pioneering spirit'.

But Len had not changed—only his place of service. Phil Booth tells of the way this 'new broom' began to sweep with great ability. 'When he came into leadership Len once more began to display his efficiency. Staff meetings which had sometimes gone on and on till the early hours of the morning now finished at nine o'clock. Up to that moment we hadn't had minutes, and we either remembered or forgot what the decisions were. We used to spend quite a bit of time chewing over what the decision had been. Not so with Len. Minutes were kept and there was a note of decisions made. Although we might alter them, at least we had a record of what they were.

'Then the offices had to be sorted out. Len eventually worked out a new system of offices with partitioning at the hostel in Upper Norwood, so if you wanted to see him you didn't have to meet him in the dining room.'

Len was always looking ahead, planning ahead, expecting more and aiming to increase the value of the work being done. Excerpts from his first letter following his appointment read as follows: 'Principles and lessons taught us by the Holy Spirit in our real experiences in India will be freely shared with the candidates; we seek to equip them spiritually to contribute to vital fellowship and to prepare them to live sacrificially. The desire for ease and plenty has permeated the church. Our stand for sacrifice is going to throw us into sharp relief, with the potential of being thought fanatical.' Len goes on, 'We are out after the young men and women of our land who enjoy a Christian life but are oblivious to its responsibilities. We are going to speak direct and straight! No frills and fancies!' And for this to be effective, 'I believe God would have us widen and intensify the prayer ministry here in HQ. Iris and I chatted yesterday about the little room next to the study being made a prayer room. A record of prayer targets would always be on the table and missionaries, staff or candidates would be free to spend time there.' He ends, 'So let us fight on and on. Already we girdle the earth. It is now to fight more and more to fight!'

Len never ceased to use his experiences in India as vital illustrations in his teaching ministry; nor did he cease to align himself with those working in other parts of the world. When speaking at a conference in 1973 his subject was, 'Are Missionaries Unbalanced?' He began by saying, 'I'm a missionary, and I pass verdict on myself this morning that I am unbalanced.' Hardly the opening to be expected from a man who was by that time International Secretary of WEC, and looked on by many as a missionary statesman. He continued, 'I started as an ordinary person, I think. I dressed like other people. I liked to watch a ball game. I liked to relax and listen to a concert of Grieg's music. I guess I was just like any other person. But even before I left home to begin missionary work I began to be different. Some admired me. They realized that I was facing high Himalayan mountains and privations for a good work, that of bringing the gospel to those in closed lands. Others pitied the missionary—look what he is leaving and the great prospects he had in his secular work. He's leaving home, father, mother, loved ones, just for a vision. He's a visionary, that's what he is. Now he's back again or she's back again after five or seven years on the mission field, and my! aren't they different now. To them some things don't seem important at all. The Ashes, Dolphins v. Redskins, Arsenal v. Wolves leave them cold. Apparently they don't see things as others see them. When they had the chance of a lifetime to meet some famous personality they showed little enthusiasm. It makes you ask where these people have been all the time. Well, where have they been?

'They have been where the conflict is with evil, and that conflict is fierce. They've been living where nice clothes don't matter because there's very little time to take care of them. They've been living where people have been dying for want of the help they could give. No doubt that one has been working where the temperature has been 120°F. in the shade—but he couldn't do his work in the shade. And time seems to have passed him by in these seven years. When you talk about the Beatles he's puzzled, and when you happen to mention the current sports personality he'll ask who he is. You just wonder how long he has been away.

'All right, how long has he been away? He's been away long enough to see thousands and thousands go into an eternity without Christ, without an opportunity to hear the gospel. That's how long he's been away. And some of those went into eternity right in front of his eyes. He saw an overcrowded Chinese ferry-boat overturn with almost a complete loss of life. He saw the mass casualties of that cholera epidemic. He saw the blood that simply ran from that Hindu-Muslim riot which broke out. How long has he been away? He's been away long enough to have two serious bouts of amoebic dysentery. He's been away long enough to nurse his wife through a very serious patch of Tarai fever in North India. He's been away long enough to have news of his mother's death, although he never heard that she was ill. And he's been away long enough to see a few Outcastes out there in India somehow respond to the love and the light and the grace of God. He's been out there long enough to feel the persecution they got from their neighbours left and right. He's identified with them, he's carried their burdens, his cheeks have been wet with their tears. He's seen them grow from just a few believers to an operating fellowship and a church, an indigenous church. A church that is mature, a church that is now sending out others to the villages around proclaiming what Christ has meant to them. That's how long he's been away.

'Yes, he's been away a long time and so he's different. Unnecessarily so now, I suppose you'll say. Yes, he's been away five or seven years, but he's back now. He might as well look to his clothes. He could get a tie with a bit of colour in it. He might take some interest in what's going on around him, and enjoy a bit of social life. Well, of course he could, but he can't forget for long that no doubt those millions are still going to a lost eternity. That new suit you think he should buy, that'd pay for 3,200 gospels when he goes back. And while you spend a day in business—just one day in business—5,000 Chinese or

91

5,000 Indians have moved over into eternity.

'And so when you meet this missionary, when he comes to your fellowship or your church, remember that he's going to be different. No doubt he's going to be unbalanced. I know you're a bit embarrassed when he's feeling for a word, but remember that for five to seven years he's been speaking another language entirely and very fluently. It could be that when he's in the pulpit he's just not the orator class. He doesn't grip you. He's a bit flat. But if you saw him in that Indian bazaar you would hear his fluency in that language; you would see the illustrations from Indian culture that he gives; you would see the crowds drinking in the words of life. He's out of place in the pulpit, no doubt, but oh, how God's anointing is upon him there in that dirty, smelly, spice-ridden bazaar in India!

'Ah yes, and when you get near him he doesn't seem to warm up so quickly as others—that youth evangelist that came, or the professor at the college—they are extrovert and you can touch them. But this chap, he doesn't warm up. Well, no doubt he doesn't. You see, for five to seven years he's been in another culture and another social structure, and he's rather unfamiliar with small talk and casual conversation.

'Are missionaries unbalanced? Of course they are. I'm one and I ought to know. But by whose scales are they unbalanced—yours, or God's?'

In words such as these, the new British Secretary of WEC used his own experience to communicate the challenge of the world's need.

CHAPTER SIX

A DISTENDED GULLET

'God, you will have to give Len a distended gullet, for he will have to swallow some big things.' Miss Annie Mitchell, who was living at the London headquarters in Upper Norwood at the time of Len's appointment, remembers that fervent prayer and how Len made a start on some of the tasks that lay ahead. 'When Len took up his new commission he walked, as it were, on his knees. There were so many different branches to the home end of the mission. Len visited them all, got his finger on the pulse of things, and made himself known to the different personalities. Many who carried responsible positions had a bit of maturity attached to them, and it was not easy for Len.'

Miss Mitchell also tells how Len sought to send out more financial support to those on the job far away. 'As soon as he became leader, God put a "burden" on his heart. The burden was to see more finance coming in for fields and missionaries. Now finance was never given priority in any meetings, except when candidates were trusting the Lord for outfit or passage. I was with Len on the finance committee, so understood why God had given him a burden. There had been no complaint from either field or missionary. But Len said to all of us, "If you feel you can join me we shall meet in the evening for prayer in the lounge." All who were free gathered. Sometimes the meetings would go on until the early hours of the morning, although we were free to leave at any time. At the very next finance meeting we were told that there had been a substantial increase in the General Fund. From that time there has been a continual increase. I always think of Len as the man who took on a burden for more finance for his fellow missionaries.'

Len refers briefly to this matter in one of his letters: 'We feel that we should see God send more to the fields through the General Fund. Extra prayer sessions will certainly be our joy and privilege as we stand with our missionaries in vital fellowship concerning their needs.'

Mary Rowe, wife of the present British Secretary, tells of her recollections of the time when Len took over the British leadership. 'I was a candidate at the time of the transition, and remember the fresh breeze of his dynamism blowing away a lot of the old traditional cobwebs! Someone commented to Norman Grubb in some alarm that we were experiencing a lot of innovations in a very short time. Generously and typically Norman Grubb laughed very heartily and said "New brooms always sweep clean—and if they are vacuum cleaners, so much the better!" That's how I remember Len. He was an efficient vacuum cleaner trying to bear patiently with his army of brooms.'

Len was very able, very ordered, very business-like, but also very human and loving and real. Lionel Hemming, the WEC surveyor and a businessman himself, shares an incident portraying this tender, caring, personal Len. 'I was new in WEC circles in those days and had not yet met Len. Wesley Driver, home on furlough from Colombia, had come to spend a week with us to take some missionary meetings in Bromley. I asked him during the week what his thoughts were of the new British Secretary. His reply was that when he and his family arrived in London by train, Len was there on the platform to welcome them home. His first action, as they got off the train and he greeted them, was to take their youngest child, then a baby, into his arms and embrace him. This little act made a deep impression on Wesley. In a moment Len had won his confidence; he realized that Len really cared.'

Although exalted to a position of great responsibility, Len deeply desired God to fit him for his task rather than settling down in his own competence. Again it is Lionel Hemming who tells us, 'At one of his first meetings at the Upper Norwood headquarters, shortly after taking the leadership, Len asked that we pray that God would give him a teachable spirit. I believe God answered that prayer in a very significant way.'

Harry Young, who now has a ministry to Asians and Arabs in Britain, tells of a lesson learned in those early days and still remembered. 'I was visiting my brother who was a candidate at WEC headquarters at the time. The day was cloudy, dull and grey and none too warm. I was making my way towards the main building when I noticed Len crossing the back yard. Suddenly he stopped, found a yard brush and set about cleaning up a lot of rubbish which had probably been deposited there by the wind.

'Had it been a candidate that responded so willingly to the need I would have been pleasantly impressed—but the man I saw in the dungarees was the Home Secretary of British WEC.

'As I got to know Len in the following years I learned

that his servant-like response to that situation was typical of him. He had learned to reflect his Master in leading by serving.'

Perhaps it was about this time that Iris began to realize that 'the man I'm married to is not the man I married'. Because Len was willing to be moulded by God, because he desired that teachable spirit, because he always reached for the highest, God was meeting Len and fashioning him after his own heart. And this came through in everything he did, from sweeping the yard to embracing babies to 'doing to others as you would like them to do to you'.

Over and over again the love of Jesus reached through Len to meet the personal needs of those around him in a way that inspired their confidence and led them to aim high in their own lives. Iain Mackenzie recalls, 'It was May of 1958 when, as a candidate, I was first introduced to Len. During the first few weeks of my time there I and another candidate had made arrangements to visit a Bible college friend in the north of London. It so happened that in the days to follow, our arrangements to visit were thrown into conflict with a surprise call for a night of prayer. I think finance and personnel were the subjects of that prayer meeting. Not wanting to disappoint the friend, we went to the visit and not to the prayer meeting. The next day Len caught me at work in the cellar. There was not much he needed to say; "Iain, I missed you at prayer last night." The sense of having let him down really hurt me. However, Len handled this so graciously; no carpeting, no telling off, just that personal sense of his being disappointed was all that was needed.

'During the course we had a visit from our Swiss WEC representatives who had come to visit some of the ladies' Bible colleges. On the day of the visit most staff members were otherwise engaged. Len was involved with some other business and there was no one and no car to take the representatives to the colleges. Following dinner that day Len and I crossed paths in the courtyard. "Iain," said Len, "can you drive?" I could, and before I knew what was behind the question he had entrusted me with his car and with the representatives. I was just a country bumpkin and knew nothing about London. I was to learn in the years to come that this was Len Moules, a man willing to entrust big things to folk like myself. All went well that day in driving and in finding the right places.

'Around that time Margaret and I came to believe that the Lord was leading us into friendship and eventually, we hoped, into marriage. It was to Len and Iris that we reported our friendship. Margaret was then doing a course in tropical diseases, but was due in HQ for final acceptance at the staff meetings. The day before she was due to arrive Len called me to his office to say that he and Iris had made arrangements for Margaret and me to use their sitting room during the staff meetings; supper would be brought to us by Iris. All this was done so that we could have a chance to share with one another. We had from 7 p.m. until 10 p.m. together for the next three nights. It was just like both Len and Iris to do this kind of thing. The trust they put into our conduct, and our responsibility, from that day on led us always to make for the highest. This is the kind of thing that I feel Len did for people; he made them reach higher as a result of the trust he had in them.'

Iain continues, 'Following my acceptance for work in Indonesia we had a long wait for our visas. Eighteen months went by and my application was turned down, and we had received no news of Margaret's. Len took time to write a word of consolation and comfort, together with a word of exhortation to stand and see God in the matter.

'We made further application for a visa and after several months of silence word came from our government representative in Java: the Indonesian government advised the engaged couple to get married and reapply for a joint visa. We were on pastoral visitation in Southampton when we had a private letter from Len and Iris in which, on behalf of the UK staff, we were asked to consider getting married.

'"If it is of any help," Len wrote, "Iris and I would like to be present—and for your guidance, we will be in the area in four weeks' time!" He and Iris were there, and their contribution remains a challenge to this day. "Let not the sun go down upon your wrath" was the basis of what Len preached at our wedding. This kind of thing was what came through to us time and again with both Len and Iris. There was a real honesty about their own lives; they lived an open book. I can still remember the morning when Len apologized to Iris at prayers over some wrong words used the day before. Walking in the light was not just an evangelical phrase. It cost him in his walk not only with Iris and his family, but also with the staff. Such a big man, such a fine man, such a lovely man had no time for sham. He was real with God and man.'

So Len began to get his roots down, encouraged and supported on all levels by Iris. One friend, Kath Wright, who attended Len's childhood church at Acton Green, tells of the place Len held in her life. 'There was some-thing outstanding about Len's personality, his mountaineering exploits, and the glamour of the mission field that made him an object of my hero worship. He was very much a part of the family of what is now called the

Memorial Free Church, and was looked on as a beloved older brother.' Kath continues, 'I think I have heard no other Bible teacher whose messages have been so enthralling as Len's. He had tremendous knowledge and an ability to make things come alive.'

A powerful illustration of this gift of Len's is a talk he gave at a missionary conference:

It is unnecessary for me to say that Paul, time and time again when needing an emphasis on some particular facet of the Christian life, looks around for an analogy which he can give. We know some of them. He sees a wrestling match and immediately he says, 'we wrestle not against flesh and blood.' He sees a boxing match and he says, 'we're not ones who go in for shadow-boxing,' and then he sees a centurion and he says, 'we are soldiers of Jesus Christ; let's put on the whole armour of God.' No doubt he's in the stadium and he sees a runner and he picks this up, 'I have run the race;' the gladiators, 'I have fought the fight.' So Paul, looking around, picks up this event and that event. I know that if he lived today he'd certainly pick up the contemporary sports that we view and which are the interest of our country; there would be something in that sport and that game which he would use as an analogy of the Christian life.

Now in 2 Corinthians 2 Paul says, 'Christ always leads us in triumph,' but there should be a slight difference here. It reads in the original, 'but thanks be to God, who in Christ, always leads us in the Triumph.' The Triumph. During his lifetime Paul must have viewed one of these great national occasions in Rome.

The highest honour a commander-in-chief could experience was that of participating in the Triumph.

A commander-in-chief didn't earn this right cheaply. In fact, no doubt many c-in-c's fulfilled their full military service and never enjoyed such an honour. And no c-in-c, as far as I understand from Roman history, ever enjoyed it twice. If you saw one Triumph in your lifetime that was all you could expect to see—it was a unique occasion.

There are some seven conditions that a commander-in-chief had to fulfil before he was granted the Triumph.

1. He had to be a full commander-in-chief, not acting.
2. He had to be engaged in a war which was not a civil war.
3. The operation had to be on foreign soil.
4. The Roman Empire must have been enlarged in territory through its military campaign—he must have gained further territory from the enemy and added it to the Roman Empire.
5. He must have brought all his troops back home and left that territory under stable Roman government.
6. He must have slain at least 10,000 of the enemy in one single engagement.
7. He must have captured either ships or great booty from the cities which had been sacked in that campaign.

From those seven conditions you can see that it was very hard for a c-in-c to claim the honour of the Triumph. It would only occur once during his military service, if ever.

This is the occasion that Paul had seen, and it so impressed him that he said, 'Yes, but we are always in victory in the Triumph of Jesus Christ.' Great thought. The spirit rises with Paul as he says 'We are always in victory, marching in the Triumph of our Lord Jesus Christ.'

Imagine that we are watching one of these Triumphs, as no doubt we have had a view of some great occasion in our own land when there were big parades through our capital city. I'll give you a running commentary of what happens when the Triumph comes through Rome on this unique and honourable occasion.

First of all we see coming towards us a group in true phalanx and in military precision, all dressed in white. These are the senators and heads of state and they are coming along that open road, flanked by the thousands at either side. They walk with the dignity which is given to this great occasion. Then, after an interval, there comes a number of men. They're carrying on their shoulders, often in pairs or fours, long poles across which are platforms, and on these platforms are great models. There's a model of the city which they surrounded or which they assaulted; they took the city after great heroism and the model gives some idea of how the soldiers took it. It could be, of course, that there was a naval engagement: then there is a model of one of the ships that was sunk so that the populace get some idea of the difficulties and the might of the enemy that opposed them. There could be a dozen of these models. Then another interval, and now men carrying poles upright with a great banner between them. On this banner is a picture. It may be a picture of how the engagement took place, or of the high passes they had to march over. It could be a picture of the armies encircling the city. Or it could be a picture of the hottest time of the engagement when heroism was at its height, so the populace know how bravely the men fought.

Now another interval and along the centre of the road, led by a girl dressed in pure white, comes a white bull. This bull is the sacrifice which is to be offered on the altar of the god or goddess of war at the conclusion of the day. So the offering is here being led along in the Triumph.

After the bull comes a pitiful sight, and it may take a long time to pass. They are the prisoners of war, men and women, dirty, bedraggled, clothes torn, chained one to another, heads bowed. They shuffle and drag themselves along, and with a clanking of chains they pass us by. There are a thousand or two thousand of them, and what a pitiful sight! If it wasn't for the fact that they had been the enemy, no doubt your heart would have been broken for them. But these are the captives, ones that had been fighting against our army. Now here they are with their just deserts, marching along in chains. These men, and some of the women too, know that when the sun sets they will die, usually by crucifixion on the trees on the hills outside Rome. They will never see the light of another day. This is their death march, with a vengeance.

Following the other prisoners come the captured generals, and how mortified they are as they walk along! A line of them, humiliated, the battle lost. They too know that this is their death march—they will not see the night.

After these prisoners and captured generals pass there is another interval, and then come the priests. The priests are dressed in white from head to foot, and each carries a silver chain with a silver incense burner at the end. The incense is burning and the censers are swung rhythmically, with the smoke pouring out. The whole of the street is filled with this pungent odour. We began to smell it before the priests arrived, but now they've passed by the heavy scent hangs in the air like a cloud over the whole proceedings. But we're soon alerted, because now comes the band. The band is playing a rhythmic military march as it moves on. Following the band comes the man we've been waiting for. There he is! He's the commander-in-chief. He's standing in his chariot and he has a driver before him. A young boy dressed in white holds the laurel wreath over his head. He's wearing a beautiful blue toga with white flecks on it, and various designs of stars which glitter as he moves.

The crowd is roaring now. The crowd is giving its plaudits, its cheers and its clapping, and he acknowledges to left and right. There he stands, the c-in-c, proud on this day. No doubt he wondered if he would ever see such a day, but the campaign is over and Rome is honouring its commander-in-chief.

Behind the c-in-c in the chariot there comes the family, all so proud. Maybe a little boy, the wife and others, basking in the honour that's given to husband and father.

Then, at a discreet interval, comes the army itself. Accoutrements have been cleaned that morning. They are shining. This army is having its day of honour. It's enjoying the glory given to its commander-in-chief. And how they walk! The precision, the swinging armour, the shields, the accoutrements shining brilliantly as the sun glints on them! There are thousands of them and the crowd roars its approval.

At last the parade has passed. The crowd surges home, having seen a sight that no doubt they'll never see again. The commander-in-chief has passed by with his Triumph.

No doubt Paul was somewhere in the crowd, and as he made his way home he said, 'This is it! This is the life we live as soldiers of Jesus Christ. We are always marching in his Triumph. We are always victorious in his train.' Then suddenly Paul switched the analogy. Lingering in his clothes is the incense, that pungent incense, and it brings him to think of this particular aspect of the Triumph. And he says, 'We are the aroma of Christ to God among those who are being saved. And we are that aroma to those who are perishing. To one the aroma of death to death, and to another a fragrance of life to life.' Paul had seen it.

As those bedraggled thousands of prisoners passed by with clanking chains and bowed heads, they smelled the incense. As that incense came up the street and enveloped them, it was the aroma of death unto death because they would never see the nightfall. They would die as the sun set. That smell was the very smell of death.

But the soldiers also smelled it as they came along behind their commander-in-chief. To them, as they marched along, it was the aroma of life unto life. It was the aroma of honour.

'Yes,' Paul says, 'that's it.' It is only one pungent smell of incense, but to one it is the aroma of death and to another the aroma of life. Paul realizes that this is exactly what our ministry is. As we are proclaiming the truths of the Lord Jesus Christ, his gospel and his claims to discipleship, it is an aroma of death to some. But to others it is an aroma of life.

Kath Wright puts an interesting poser when she questions, 'I wonder to what use Len's gifts and abilities might have been put had he not become a Christian? Even as a Christian they might have been wasted and half-used had he not been totally dedicated and sold out

103

to God. He was such an utterly joyous man who communicated to Christian and non-Christian alike and had a tremendous rapport with young people. I find it very difficult to put into words the real depth of his life and teaching, except to say that he was the most real Christian I have ever known. He was a living proof that God is, and that God does change lives, and that God will get the best out of any life yielded to him.'

It was to Kath Wright that Len gave the privilege of joining him on television, when asked to appear by the same man who had interviewed him earlier on radio.

Len's reaction to this new life is expressed in the closing words of his letters: 'It's going to be tough if we are going to be vital for God, so, a tough year for everyone!'; or 'Yours Crusading with a thrill'; or 'Cheerily in him, Len and Iris'.

And it was tough, very tough at times. Len shares that one year 'the first few months of the year ushered in a period of tragedy and yet really of triumph'. One after another, as Len puts it, 'answered the Lord's sudden call to glory.' But knowing where each one was going brought joy instead of sorrow. 'Thus, in heaven's battlements, the crowd of witnesses grows apace. They will soon need WEC hymn-books up there!' Len writes. In case anyone should feel this to be flippant, Mrs Margaret Barron knew that there was only love in the remark. 'When I stood by the bedside of my husband after he had gone home I said, "Another WEC hymn-book."' She adds, 'I shall never forget that when I came back to England from the Gambia, Len was at the station to meet me. He never spoke, just put an arm round me and put me in the car to take me to headquarters. He knew I had a sore heart as I left a grave out there. I shall never forget his and Iris's loving kindness to me.'

CHAPTER SEVEN

LIQUID GLORY

As the world and WEC and Len moved towards a new decade, a new expectancy hung in the air. Len confesses sadly, 'I came home in 1948 and looked around the world, and there was hardly a ripple of revival. I came home after twenty years of ministry away in the Himalayas on the Tibetan border with so little to show. I believed God's word would not return void, but there was so little to see.'

At the end of this new decade, however, there would be a note of joy and excitement: 'The Spirit has brought many things. As I've watched over the decade of the 1960s I've seen a new measure of worship, I've seen a new dimension of love, I've seen the Spirit bringing new truths and new aspects. And the Spirit as it flows in the word of God has been redemptive every time. I've been enriched. I thank God I live in these days.' But there were to be joys and sorrows, light and deep darkness, the familiar routine and exciting changes before Len would look back in this way.

As the new decade approached, God performed one of many miracles that were to come as shafts of light as the days passed. In one of Len's letters he writes, 'We often get inspiration from seeing Fran and Elsie Rowbotham pursue the conference centre they desire so much.' One day the phone rang and Fran Rowbotham picked it up. '"You've been looking at a property up there on the west coast of Scotland; what do you think of it?" It was Len's voice on the phone, speaking from our London head-quarters to me in Glasgow.

'We had looked over this property and grounds, but the price was way beyond what we could pay. My reply to Len was, "Yes, we have looked over the property, the three acres of grounds and the other buildings, but we have turned it down in our minds." Next came the question, "Will you take it as a gift?" I gasped, "What?" "Yes," said Len, "the owner is a Christian. When he knew we were interested in it and the purpose for which we would use it, he decided to make it a gift to the mission if we would like it. What are we going to do about it?" "Len, we're going to accept it," I replied.

'Ever since then Kilcreggan has been the holiday conference centre of WEC, and year by year Len was a great figure in the conferences. It was his delight to be in the midst of the whole programme. His messages from the platform and his Bible ministry were used to challenge and deepen the experience of very many people.'

The generosity of such an outstanding gift must have echoed in Len's own heart. Often he was like Peter and John who met the man crippled from birth and gave him what he most needed, healing in Jesus' name, not the silver or gold which he had expected. Len was always in the giving business—giving time, giving love, giving his talents and expertise. And he was very, very practical. Bob Hiley, a close friend of Len and Iris and later General Secretary of CLC (Christian Literature Crusade), tells of the time Len stayed with them when he was on the road taking meetings.

'We had an old radio which didn't work until Len got his hands on it. He roared with laughter when we told him that now we had a radio that worked we also had a new problem—we didn't have a licence or the money to buy one! No problem to Len. He produced the licence—paid up.'

Bob and Ada gave to Len in turn and had a surprise which eventually enriched them. 'We always gave visitors a book or two before they left Leicester. Imagine my surprise when we asked Len to pick a couple and he asked for any of Boreham's essays. Boreham, I thought, fancy Len wanting books we can't sell! "But," said Len, "Boreham puts flesh on the bones." After he left us I took up Boreham and have never put him down again. I am hooked!'

It was some years later, when Bob Hiley had been appointed General Secretary of CLC, that he went to Len with some really difficult problems. As he shared them with Len, tears began to flow. Then Bob broke down and they wept together. Neither spoke until Len wiped his eyes and said, 'That's really all I have to say to you.' He had said everything.

Some of the problems facing Len as British leader were not at all easy to resolve. The story behind Jim Rodger's determination to obey God and serve him in what is now Zaire is told by Len himself.

'It's a miracle that Jim ever got to the mission field. He came to our WEC headquarters as a candidate three times, and three times he was turned down. Academically he was brilliant. He had a Master of Arts degree with Honours in Languages; from many aspects we couldn't have had a better candidate. But what do you do with a man who goes down and gets on a bus and then

107

forgets where he's going? He has to get off to collect his senses as to why he's there and where he is going. On three occasions that happened. Once or twice he got on a bus and had to get off again, and on the third occasion he got to the bus stop and wondered why he was there, having forgotten completely what was his intended journey that day. Well, this isn't missionary material, really, is it? Although he had a deep love for Africans and was an accomplished, certified school teacher with an honours degree—well, that's all very well, but these other things are very very real indeed. I didn't think we could send a man out to the heart of Africa who had lapses of memory as drastic as this. And so the third time we said, "Jim, we're afraid not. You just look to the Lord to find some appointment at home."

'But do you know, the field heard that we had three times turned down a man who was determined to get to Congo, as we called it then. We like men and women who get their teeth into a call and say, "I don't care what you say, I'm going, and if you don't accept me I'm going on my own."

'Jim came back the third time and said, "I know God has called me. God's called me to Congo and I'm going." And the WEC staff said, "We're sorry, but we think it would be far better if you stayed at home." Well, the missionaries in Congo heard this and said, "We want a man who's come three times to WEC headquarters and said he's going to the Congo, whom you've turned down. We want this man and we'll take every responsibility." I wrote back, "All right, it's all on your heads. If he's not satisfactory or anything like that, you've only yourselves to blame. We warned you. When he gets there he may wonder why he's out there. He has lapses of memory."

'Well, Jim went out. And Jim loved the Africans and

the Africans loved him from the day he arrived. If ever a home staff were wrong, we were wrong over Jim Rodger.'

It was to be only a short while before pressure began to mount on all sides. Writing in January 1961, Len devotes a considerable portion of his letter to the unrest in Congo. There was considerable movement of personnel from all missions, and Len says at the close of his letter that six mission stations were by then unmanned and many of the missionaries had been brought home. But not Jim Rodger.

A decade later Len spoke on the challenge of our circumstances, centring on Christ's words, 'What shall I say? "Father, save me from this hour"? No, for this purpose I have come to this hour' (John 12:28). Len spoke of Jim Rodger and a young American, Bill McChesney. He told how he visited Zaire at Christmas-time, 1971. 'Eventually I arrived at Wamba. Oh, what a welcome! The crowds were waiting for us; they ran beside the Land Rover. We went in under the garlanded arch, and very soon we were unpacking our kit outside a little rest house. It seemed as if it had seen better days, and the missionary in charge said, "C. T. Studd built this." I could believe it! But the next words sombred me: "Bill and Jim spent their last night in this room." I put up the camp bed. I lay on my back on that bed in that room. "Bill and Jim spent their last night here." If only these walls could speak. If only they could tell me what went through the men's minds. Just outside on that little veranda there had been a Simba guard, daubed from head to foot with mud mixed with the blood of animals. He was hideous in appearance, standing outside with a spear, waiting for any opportunity or excuse to impale them. And inside were Bill and Jim, possibly knowing it was their last night on earth. What could these walls tell me? Bill McChesney was an American, but Jim Rodger was a Scotsman. The American was almost under the sentence of death already, but not the Scotsman. The nationals were against the Belgians and the Americans at that time, but those of different nationalities were given a few days reprieve. Bill must have known that this was his last night on earth. And Jim? Jim had promised Bill, who wasn't too well, "Bill, I'll never leave you. I'll be at your side right through to the end."

'I was sleeping that night in a room where they had spent their last night. I can't help but feel that these words were in Jim's mind: "Father save me from this hour? No! For this purpose I have come to this hour. Father, glorify thy name."

'The next morning I went down to the local prison. The prison officer opened it up. I walked into the yard. There was the spot where the line of prisoners had stood that day. Jim and Bill were in that line. It was on this very spot, as I stood in the middle of that prison yard, that the command was given, "Belgians and Americans, one step forward." Jim Rodger, the Scot, stepped forward side by side with Bill, whom he would never leave. One of the Roman Catholic priests there said, "But he is a . . .". The words weren't heard in the Simbas' cries as they fell on Jim and Bill. They were knocked to the ground and, where I was standing, they were trodden on until they were disembowelled.

'Later that afternoon I stood on the bridge and was told, "The bodies were thrown down there." I am a man, and sometimes we feel that tears should be foreign to a man, but my eyes were wet that day.

'I lay in that room. I stood in that prison square. I went to the bridge. And I followed the footsteps of a man who

110

said, "Father, save me from this hour? No, for this purpose I have come to this hour.'"

Len had to learn this submission himself, and he found it hard. Once, when talking of the cost of discipleship to Jesus Christ, Len asked, 'Is there anyone here whose heart is in rebellion against the circumstances you are in? If so, this is death to you. Is there anyone here who has been through trying, even overwhelming circumstances, but you've accepted them and the Lord has brought you through? If you are singing praise and thanks to God in the middle of such things, then this is life to you. I know what I'm talking about.

'I came home in 1956 only for furlough, longing, longing to get back to the Tibetan border to that beloved work. In October 1956 the staff unanimously asked me and my wife to remain behind as director of the work in Britain. I said, "No!" Well, we didn't agree. Three months went by and there was another conference and on the first day of the conference they again unanimously asked my wife and me to accept the directorship of the work in Britain. I said, "No! I'm going back to the Tibetan border." But often, you know, your wife senses what is the Lord's will before you do. On the second day I said, "No!" again. But on the third day my wife said to me, "Why don't you capitulate, Len? You know it's the Lord's will." And then I accepted what I knew to be the will of God. But deep within I accepted it grudgingly. For four years I did a job which I knew to be the Lord's will, and yet I rebelled against it. It was not to me the sweet and acceptable will of God. Deep inside it was death to me.

'In 1961 the rebellion in my heart affected me mentally and physically. I was almost at a breakdown and God said, "The trouble is that you are at war with my will." I

111

said, "Yes, I am, Lord. You know I want to be back on the Tibetan border instead of going around here in Britain. I'm strong. Still years ahead of me. What am I doing back here?" The Lord said, "I want you here. And it is the sweet and acceptable will of God."

'And that day I broke. I said, "All right, Lord. Please make it the acceptable will of God to me. I give up the field. I release it with all its thoughts and callings. And my love for it, Lord—I put that on the altar. I put it on the cross. I accept this from your hand." From that moment there was peace. When there was peace there was physical health and mental strength. There were new resources, spiritual resources, and I knew again the joy of the Lord. And this was life to me.'

With this new life Len continued to hold the reins of a tremendous diversity of matters, many of which could have been considered a full-time occupation. He reported with joy the refurbishing of Kilcreggan and the Lord's supply of finance to Fran and Elsie Rowbotham. He kept up the search for a home for retired missionaries. He reported on staff health, visa situations, the comings and goings of personnel; on exhibitions, on situations abroad where WEC workers were stationed. He even found time to write and have published his own book on the years in the Himalayas. And he told with eagerness of the search for property for yet another offshoot of WEC, Radio Worldwide.

Following the first field leaders' conference to be held at Kilcreggan in 1961, Len's name was put forward for the duties of International Secretary. This would give him the responsibility for WEC work worldwide. He once said, 'If you feel you cannot take any more on your plate, the only thing you can do is to get a bigger plate!' However, the nomination was not ratified at this point, when some sixty WEC leaders gathered for a month of fellowship and planning.

According to Len, 28th February 1962 was 'the darkest day of my life'. It was probably said with his tongue in his cheek, but that day was Len's fiftieth birthday, and he found his half-century a big pill to swallow. Up to the eyes in activity of all kinds, the zeal within him needed a limitless future to cope with the challenges which came at him from all sides.

With his ever broadening vision, Len reported on places of unrest overseas. Congo, 'a situation of deep concern;' Vietnam, where the ugly head of conflict was rising; Chad; France; Thailand; each found a place before the routine reports on the many and varied demands in Britain.

Iris, too, was 'seeking a bigger plate', as she had to add the work of the kitchen to her many duties until the right person came along to fill the need. One particular concern of hers was the welfare of the missionaries' children. She desired to stand in prayer for them for their specific needs and, when possible, to meet with others for this purpose.

Their own young people were growing up fast. Noel had left school and by sixteen was happily working on Uncle Willie's turkey farm prior to studying for his Poultry Husbandry Certificate at agricultural college. Carol was at boarding school in lovely North Wales, while Beth attended a local school and lived in the hurly-burly of headquarters.

Older young people in the form of candidates were also milling around during their four months' candidates' course. In February 1962, Len tells us, 'we had an all-time record of thirty-three candidates in headquarters.' All these additional people to house and feed brought a

113

whole new set of problems with regard to accommodation. Len was constantly revamping the house layout and attempting to squeeze yet another sardine into the proverbial tin.

Is it any wonder that Phil Booth reports, 'Len always wanted more room at headquarters in Highland Road. We used to talk over all kinds of plans for building here and extending there, putting another floor on that or this or the other; but it all led to nothing.'

1963 was Jubilee Year for WEC and a very busy year for all concerned. Fifty years had passed since C. T. Studd had left home, an invalid wife and four daughters to obey the call to work in Africa. Some might ask, what can one man do? And the answer is that he can inspire many others to follow him in a life of complete sacrifice and glorious satisfaction. Speaking in the 1970s, Len tells of the times when he first knew the mission, and the method of commemoration they chose for their founder, C. T. Studd.

'The Crusade is one of the largest interdenominational, international missions in the world. But there was a time in 1931 when people were quite willing to wash their hands of this Crusade; in fact, it wasn't good to mention WEC. We had gone through a crisis. Our founder, C. T. Studd, had been buried. There had been a tremendous division with the loss of personnel and of fields, and WEC was *persona non grata*. Some good Christian men and women considered us to be an irresponsible mission. But in early 1932 it was my privilege as a young man to begin to feel the winds that were blowing through headquarters, though I wasn't associated with WEC at that time. I was an electrical engineer putting electric light in some of the houses, and I was in on morning prayers. I remember, laughingly, the morning prayers in which

114

they were wondering whether they should have a memorial to C. T. Studd. And one or two of those present thought of putting a plaque on the wall. I remember Norman Grubb saying, "Plaque on the wall! If C. T. Studd were to see a plaque on the wall he'd rise from the dead and tear it down." He was almost Churchillian in his aggression.

'Eventually we knew that the only memorial to C. T. Studd which he, in glory, would give approval to, was a living memorial of dedicated men and women out on the mission field.

'We had what was called a Memorial Ten. In 1932 we were even lower then than we are now, and Social Security and social amenities were not then as they are now. The food lines, the unemployed, the out of work, the value of the pound; one could go on. They were desperate days. Missionary societies were selling properties overseas and retrenching to a minimum which they could keep up, and not sending any reinforcements to the field until the economic conditions changed. Any mission that sent out reinforcements was irresponsible under the financial conditions of those early 1930s.

'When God told WEC to send out ten in 1932 as a memorial, we thought, let's keep quiet and tell them we've done it after they are out! But as our anointed brother, Norman Grubb, led us through our studies at morning prayers, he showed us that when God told his prophets to do something they said what was *going* to be done. Rain was going to fall, or famine was going to come, or there wouldn't be any rain. They didn't wait till afterwards and say, "I told you so. I knew that was going to happen." They declared it. They staked all on God. And we've got to do the same.

'So we put in print that we were going to send out ten

115

missionaries in one year. How irresponsible can an organisation be? And more than that, we told the field leader in Zaire to be prepared for ten new missionaries coming out. Before those missionaries were in headquarters to be tested and sent out, the field leader was on reconnaissance to open new stations for the ten that hadn't arrived.

'Now you know why WEC means, "Where Everybody's Crazy!" There are grounds for it. But by the end of the year nine were in and some had gone to the field. God was sending in the men and women and God was sending in the money.

'But we had said that God would give us ten in a year. Oh, when the last days of the year were coming and there was one more needed and hardly anyone on the horizon! Was God going to give us the ten in the year? But if God is God then the ten would come within the year.

'There was a conference at the Swansea Bible College. It was the end of the conference and Norman Grubb was speaking. One dear man had just finished his training, was leaving within twenty-four hours, and didn't know where he was going. He'd had no guidance at all. He didn't go to the final meeting. He thought he should have time with the Lord, so he lay down on his tummy behind a rhododendron bush with his Bible, reading and praying.

'When he heard the last hymn being sung he got up, went across, and waited for the speakers to come out. Eventually Norman Grubb came out and saw the student standing there. He went up to him and put his hand on his shoulder. "Praise God," he said. "God told me you were the tenth." They talked, and there was a witness in the student's soul that he was the tenth. When they'd talked a man came up to Norman Grubb and said, "Has

116

he offered?''

'''Yes.''

'''Then here's a cheque to send him out to Zaire.''

'The next year it was fifteen and after that twenty-five. In the thirties the Spirit of God was moving mightily in aggressive faith.'

If that was the spirit of the thirties, then the Jubilee Year of 1963 could only be a year of outreach to challenge others to obey if God called. The year began with Len and Iris still being recommended to carry the responsibility of International Secretary as well as that of British Secretary, as no one had been appointed to take over that position. But Len was well aware of the size of the task. He wrote, 'Before we felt free to stand for confirmation in the appointment, we needed to confess that the pace had been hard and the responsibilities heavy. The inspiration of the position had ebbed. It was obvious to Iris and me that the load had to be considerably lightened. We suggested that a couple be appointed to look after the total welfare of the candidates. This had been a realized need for two years, but nothing had been done to meet it. The staff were wonderful in realizing the importance of the whole case, and were good enough to ask Eric and Daisy Smith to undertake this very important task.'

Meanwhile, Britain survived a mini ice-age in the early months of the WEC Jubilee Year. Len says that 'it was in this snow-bound Britain that the Jubilee team with their exhibition ventured out on a very ambitious programme. Jack Aitken with the Bedford Utilabrake, and I with the Vanguard Estate, faced fog, snow and ice with bitter winds. It was difficult to get the halls warm and folk were reluctant to come out on the treacherous roads. But in spite of it all we experienced grand times of blessing.'

117

For six weeks during the summer of 1963 Len and a team transported the Jubilee exhibition to Scandinavia and other parts of Europe. There they were met by packed churches and enthusiastic hearers. Is it to be wondered at that 1964 began with a backlog of weariness and physical strain? As Len put it, 'Now it's all over — Jubilee Year, that is — and we feel strangely tired out!'

At home a search was started for new accommodation. Again it is Phil Booth who tells us how the Lambeth Borough Council put a match to the fire by issuing a compulsory purchase order on all seven properties that made up the WEC headquarters: 'We used to wander round and visit places, but nothing clicked. Eventually the compulsory purchase order came through and this really was God's signal and God's time. Immediately a map of the surroundings of London was brought out and a circle drawn on it. That circle indicated the boundary of the tuppenny telephone call in those days, and the idea was that somewhere on that circle there should be a place for us. After a bit more thinking Len favoured the north-west: it was near the M1 and, prospectively, the M4 as well, though the M4 wasn't yet in being at the time.'

Len himself comments, 'We shall be granted market value compensation on the properties, but we do not know how much we will get. What are we going to do, and when? It looks as if we shall be moving before the end of 1965.'

Meanwhile the work had to continue, and there was great personal concern over WECcers in several parts of the world. In the early part of the year an attempt was made on the lives of Roy Spraggett and his family out in Vietnam. Roy says, 'Our home was destroyed after being mined. It happened early in the morning and the news

118

got back to England later that day. My brother-in-law, at that time a chef at a hotel, heard the news very late at night and had the notion to phone WEC headquarters at half-past twelve in the morning. At that unearthly hour the phone rang only once, and there was Len answering. He had a compassion which involved his whole life.'

And in that year of 1964 Len began the travels that were to be the pattern of his coming years. He visited Scotland again in March to lecture at the college and visit 'The Elms', where the missionaries' children made their home. And there was Kilcreggan and the Press. Len and Iris returned from Scotland in time to fly to the States for three weeks. Len spent two of those weeks in conference with the Co-ordinating Council of WEC at Fort Washington, Pennsylvania. From there Len and Iris flew on to Minneapolis to visit the Bethany Fellowship for 'a long weekend of blessing and inspiration'. Home again, and then Len was off to Council meetings in France for a few days.

But it was a longer tour that was to dominate Len's year. He was asked by Norman Grubb to stand in for him for two weeks' meetings in Johannesburg. Len had a deep concern for workers in that great continent, and 'it was felt I should not fly over Chad and Congo, but descend to have time with our workers.' So the tour was planned with ten days in Chad and three weeks in different parts of Congo, followed by the ministry in South Africa.

Len set off on 13th August, planning to return on 7th October in time for the WEC Annual Rally on Saturday, 10th October. But he was to be disappointed over his proposed visit to Congo, as he was strongly advised not to attempt to enter the country. In the end he was put down at Brazzaville on Monday, 7th September, and found to his concern that there was no plane to Johannesburg until Friday, the 11th.

'In the hotel I spent a great deal of time on my knees before the Lord, particularly to know a new touch from him. I desired to be a channel cleansed and anointed for the particular service ahead of me. Do understand me when I say that there was one hour in which I almost struggled with the Lord for something further for this coming ministry. A new touch, a new anointing, a new outpouring of power was my desire. Once I found myself gripping the blanket and pulling it towards me as I wrestled and cried to God to come upon me again. I was willing for anything if he would only come in in his own way. Later in the afternoon, still on my knees, I heard a voice as clearly as if someone were kneeling beside me saying, "Len, I am in you and with you—what more do you need?" It came a second time. I knew it was the Lord. He had answered my prayer. With spontaneous thanks and praise I rose to my feet confident that the coming weeks would be ones in which his purposes would be reached and achieved to his glory.'

And what a blessing Len experienced in every way! God came by his Spirit into every meeting during those two weeks. 'The simple messages were translated into Zulu and Basutu, and were taken by the Holy Spirit deep into the lives of all of us. Broken prayers with tears were wonderful to hear. I had not heard such prayers before.' At the close of Len's stay he writes, 'My heart was very full. Tears were not far from my eyes when I shook hands with Hans and Letty von Staden. We had seen God answer their prayers. He had poured out his Spirit upon us. I don't think any of us could be the same again.'

Back home, however, many of the same concerns were still to the fore, the property being perhaps one of the most dominant.

And all the time the Congo Rebellion was still a day-to-day concern. News of the ill-treatment of missionaries from all missions by the Simba rebels filtered through. Rumour was rife. One report would state that many had been massacred, the next that all were safe. Eventually the picture became clear. All had suffered psychological and emotional trauma, and several had received physical violence. Four had lost their lives and one was missing. Among those who died were Jim Rodger and Bill McChesney, whose deaths were reported in *The Daily Telegraph*, as well as Cyril Taylor of New Zealand and Muriel Harman of Canada. Missing was Winnie Davis, and the suspense as to her whereabouts was to continue for a further eighteen months.

In 1967 Len reported, 'It could not help but be a shock at first. It was inconceivable that Winnie should not come through. But God deemed otherwise, and reflection confirms to us that this was the redemptive, victorious climax. Father Alphonse Strijbosch, a Dutch Roman Catholic priest who escaped, told us that Winnie had been fairly well treated, but was very emaciated and had few clothes. She had lived with the ten wives of the rebel General Gaston Ngalo, who had often promised her his protection until she was free to return to Europe. Although a prisoner, Winnie maintained medical work and evangelistic services right up until the last. On 24th May, (1967) a National Congolese Army reserve column got very near to them. For three days the rebel remnant of less than a hundred walked and walked, deeper into the jungle. They had hardly any food except a little elephant meat and rodents at night. On Saturday, the 27th, they crossed rivers and struggled through deep jungle. About 10.00 a.m. Father Strijbosch saw Winnie lying by the path. He thought she was resting but then saw that she was dead, with knife wounds in her head and neck and blood on her mouth. She had been dead about fifteen minutes, not more. A few minutes later he was rescued by National Congolese Army troops.'

To add to the deep concern and burden of responsibility Len was carrying, a further spanner was thrown in the works due to a protest over the compulsory purchase order. This led to the Minister of Housing in Parliament adjusting the order so that the line ran right down Highland Road. This no doubt helped many private householders but it left WEC in a very difficult position, as half their property was now under the order and half was released.

Jock Purves tells us, 'At meeting after meeting we considered all that this would mean in acquiring another set of buildings suitable as a home base. There was much to think about, pray and confer about, work for and become decisive on.' All this was added to a 'normal' overload of work pressing a man already deeply weary.

As one of a team, though admittedly head of the team, there was no way that Len could move forward without discussion, consultation, persuasion and pressures. Suddenly it was too much.

One day Len did not appear at a staff meeting and Iris went to find him. She discovered him on his knees by his bed, chewing at his pyjamas, tearing them with his teeth, and almost going out of his mind. The pressures, the problems, the difficulties, and the frustrations had been forced within, and something had to give. 'Uncle' Frank Martin of Len's Galatians 2:20 experience was in the country, and was told so urgently of the situation that he prayed all morning. Iris, attacked by thoughts that she had urged Len to carry the heavy load of responsibility, thought he had gone out of his mind through her pushing him. Now she lay on the bed with him in her arms and hugged him to her each time he seemed to reach a crisis of terrible tension and overwhelming panic.

What should they do? Eventually Iris phoned Dr Q. Muriel Adams, Len's contemporary at the Missionary School of Medicine in 1935 and by this time a Harley Street consultant. Dr Adams was so concerned that she was ready to cancel all appointments and go to Len at once, but as the immediate crisis eased it was arranged that Len should be taken to Harley Street.

Dr Adams tells us that 'this reaction is the penalty for being a sensitive person'. She tells us, 'people thought Len did things easily, but this was not so. He was very very sensitive, and minded about things very much. He was a person who cared, who didn't like pitting his will against others, who never found it easy to speak out when he didn't agree with someone and would lose sleep in the agony of facing a person over something. This time the tensions had been repressed until something gave way. Len even kept things from Iris in order not to worry her.'

The outcome was a session on the mechanics of the autonomic nervous system, with instruction on preventing the system from getting out of control and strict instruction to Iris to make Len her first priority at all times.

There was to be another crisis closely connected to this experience, a crisis that was to change Len's life and open his eyes wide to the power of God through the Holy Spirit. This crisis was so real and so precious to Len that he spoke of it only rarely. He gave an account of it only two months before he died: 'I had my head in my hands up in my office in Highland Road, Upper Norwood,

Crystal Palace. I'd come to the end of my tether. I could not go on. I felt like giving up, and yet was reluctant to do that.

'At that time there had come into the candidates course a young man called Jim. And when that young man came in, with him came a dimension of spiritual life that I have very seldom known since. I loved to hear Jim pray and share, and when he wasn't praying or sharing he walked about as the very essence of Jesus himself. That candidate had a dimension of spiritual power I didn't have: And here I was, British Secretary, with twenty years' missionary experience under my belt. I sat one night with my head in my hands, and the Holy Spirit said to me,

'"Call for Jim."

'"Sorry, Lord, what did you say?"

'"Call for Jim."

'"But, Lord, the British Secretary doesn't call for a candidate to give him spiritual counselling."

'"Call for Jim."

'"Yes, Lord, I know he could help, bless him—but there is position, there is status, Lord. You don't ask candidates to pray with British Secretaries."

'"Call for Jim."

'We had an internal phone so I dialled down to a room below.

'"Is Jim about?" Of course, God had arranged for Jim to be about. He was going to help. Jim walked into my office, and as a big brother to a little brother I poured out my heart to him. Jim was young, a candidate, yet so mature. When I'd finished, with my head in my hands, he said, "Let's pray." The next moments are sacred; I don't like to share them with anybody. But they concluded with a touch from his hands on my head, and a

124

prayer of such Holy Ghost initiation came from his lips that an experience of fire went through me. God met me that night in a new dimension of his Holy Spirit.'

Len comments on the difference this experience made in his life: 'Things have changed since that day. I have been confronted with aspects of demonic possession—almost every week we face a problem like this. Dear ones, I humbly share this as only a sinner saved by grace; the Lord has chosen that he, with all authority, should live in us and through us always, until our travelling days are done. I find that that authority works. These days that precious name of Jesus has authority and I can sing, and mean it, that "At the name of Jesus, devils fear and flee". And they do. Praise be to his name.'

It was a different Len who rose from his knees that evening—an ordinary man who had experienced an extraordinary touch from God. It was so real and so vital that he confessed that 'even his position in the mission would have to take second place to the light the Lord had given and the blessing he had been granted'. From that day Len knew without a shadow of doubt that the filling and gifts of the Holy Spirit set out in the Scriptures were God's provision for his own as they lived in the world. A new power, a new authority and a new anointing entered Len's experience.

Another result of that crisis evening in Len's life was that he saw the world with new understanding. He had looked for revival areas before, objectively, but now it was his delight to learn of the outpouring of the Spirit of God in any part of the world. He began to amass a dossier to share with others to the praise and glory of God.

CHAPTER EIGHT

A DEPOSIT OF GOD

From the time Len took on the British leadership of WEC, he was totally committed to a multitude of both mission and other concerns and activities. He was on this board and that board; his advice was sought in many directions. He was urged to throw the weight of his experience into the work of the EMA (the Evangelical Missionary Alliance) and considered it 'my privilege to give the right hand of fellowship to the secretary of a Pentecostal society and welcome him into the body of evangelical societies of the EMA'.

Time was at a premium, but the request to take on the international leadership of WEC was still before Len. About this Len says, 'During the staff meetings we needed to consider the possibility of our successors in British leadership, in view of the possibility of our being called by WEC International in confirmation of Norman Grubb's nomination of us. However, after a great deal of prayer and wide consideration there appeared to be as yet no couple upon whom God was signally putting his hand to fill this appointment. Equal in strength was the conviction that our time here was not yet finished, and that we should continue. Thus the vital decision was placed at our door, to be made personally. After prayer and talking together we only got the peace we sought when we decided to ask Rubi (Norman Grubb) to make another nomination, as we were unable as yet to relinquish British leadership.'

Some months later Len writes, 'In my earlier letter I mentioned the attitude Iris and I had, and the decision we had made, regarding our nomination for International Secretaryship. It would be impossible to comment on all the correspondence that has gone to and fro from the many concerned. But we did feel eventually that the Lord would ask us to accept the nomination, and to accept it together with that of the British responsibility for the time being. The British home base are praying and quietly looking to the Lord for our successors here in Britain, and we are sure that the Lord will give us the enabling to fulfil the increasing responsibility.'

The enabling Len and Iris received from the Lord was very much the outworking of Len's experience of the Holy Spirit's power coming upon him. With the new power came a new love, and as Len learned of this new love he gave teaching, encouragement and warning on several occasions. 'As I dwell on this spiritual experience in the word of God, how wonderful it is that the chapter of love is sandwiched between 1 Corinthians 12 and 14. We cannot proceed from the gifts of the Spirit in chapter twelve to the gifts of the Spirit in chapter fourteen without going through the anointing of love. This experience (of the Holy Spirit) can either enrich us or prejudice the strong bonds of fellowship in Christ that we cherish so much. Those who have been so enriched should beware of a spirit of pride, or of showing a sense of authority which some feel is synonymous with this experience. If anything this anointing is an anointing of love and must manifest itself in meekness, lowliness and brokenness. So let pride and prejudice be gone and crucified; and may love and consideration for one another, in sincere tenderness of another's opinion, take its place to melt us and weld us in a unity we've never known before.'

Another time Len warned against expecting God to do things today the same way that he did them in the past. 'I'm a bit chary when people say, "God always. . . ." May I give you a word of warning? Be careful when you say that: God does not "always". It is so easy for us to try and contain God in an equation, $A + B = C$. God never works like that. God is going to work how he will, when he will and through whom he will, and no one will say him nay.

'I will share a word of warning: I believe that when God moves in revival in this country—and he will—there will be aspects of this revival that will be difficult for us to accept. Be very cautious in criticizing the intentions, the methods, the objectives and the ways of God and who he uses. Did not Gamaliel say, far better keep silent because it may be of God?'

One aspect of God's move was to suffer criticism and misunderstanding from many. It was that God by his Holy Spirit was able to reach and restore young people who sought their thrills and highs through the drug trail. In order to get alongside these young folk, God sometimes gave extraordinary training to people in order to make them acceptable to the addicts. One such was Vic Ramsey, now of Red House rehabilitation centre for addicts. Vic tells us his story:

'I'd come through a very traumatic experience, and I'd resigned from the ministry and said I'd never preach again. I'd been in business as well as in the ministry, and it all collapsed around me and I found myself serving a short jail sentence. During that time I felt God drawing me to troubled people, and I didn't know what to do. I asked the Lord who I should go and see to talk these things over. It was then that I was given Len's name as one to go to for advice. We lived only a stone's throw from each other. We began to talk about how the Holy Spirit had dealt with my life, and I shared my testimony. Len asked me if I'd come and share my story with the students and the HQ staff at morning prayers. That introduced me properly, and I got close to Len and felt I was getting friendly with a spiritual giant. All I wanted to do was to draw from him. He always made me feel that I was the only one in the world that he was speaking to. I walked out ten feet, twenty feet, tall after coming away from Len.

'I could tell from the way he was talking to me that although he had a multitude of things to think about, he was concentrating on me. He always left a deposit of God with me. He had a way of helping me turn my problems into plans. When I was really up against it he would draw from an encyclopedia of experiences that made me realize I was talking to one of God's statesmen.

'He used an expression to me that I'll never forget, and that is that "ministry is caught more than it's taught".

'Len helped me to see that stumbling blocks could be stepping stones, and that even my time in jail should be used as one of life's investments. Surely there was a man sent from God whose name was Len Moules.'

So Len's busy life went on. Always there was some special event lying ahead, frequently some crisis to attend to. Meanwhile there was the multitude of mission tentacles to keep unravelled.

1966 saw an All-British WEC Conference in March;

new houseparents, Leslie and Pam Potter, to The Elms; Billy Graham's crusade with many staff working as advisors and counsellors; and still the touch of blessing at headquarters.

In August Len and Iris were at Kilcreggan for two weeks before Len went on his own to the States, where he was to attend conferences at WEC headquarters at Camp Hill, Fort Washington, and at Bethany Fellowship. 'Iris was unable to accompany me on my short but eventful visit to the USA. The temperature in New York was well over 100°F. when Dave Cornell met me at Philadelphia Airport. Even the tar on the roads was picking up as we drove to Camp Hill. The famous airline strike also had its effect. I'm so grateful for all that our North American Crusaders did to get me to Bethany Fellowship in Minneapolis. At 3.30 one morning we left Fort Washington by car with two drivers to start the 1,200-mile journey halfway across America. We only stopped en route for petrol and to change drivers, and it was about 1.30 the next morning when we drove into Bethany. On our arrival we found that Ted Hegre (Founder Director of Bethany Fellowship) had been held up in Brazil and my colleague on the conference platform had been delayed in New York. To cut a long story short, I batted alone from Sunday until Wednesday night when Ted Hegre arrived. My fellow speaker did not arrive until Friday night, and the conference ended on Sunday! But the Lord was pleased to bless, and on more than one occasion the communion rail was filled with young and old seeking the Lord in a new way. Just before we started out on the return journey the tornado season broke on us, and one afternoon the clouds began to circle over Bethany. Soon the father and mother of a twister touched down about four or five miles away, causing considerable damage.

'The conference at Camp Hill was one I'm glad I did not miss. To meet so many missionaries was more than a mere coincidence. God met us in a measure of blessing which seemed to reach a peak during a night of prayer, when in melting and brokenness the Lord walked in our midst.'

Ted Hegre wrote of Len, 'I first met Len at Abbot Mount in the foothills of the Himalayas. Whether he was there, at Bethany, or at his home base in London, he was always the same. He was a joyous Christian and one who inspired confidence. He was a man who knew God and one who could be trusted. He was not afraid to try the impossible. He knew the Bible well because he knew the Author. Besides all that, Len was great fun. He was an enjoyable person. Visits with him were always delightful as well as edifying. I considered Len one of my best friends. I know I will see him again—and many others too, because of his faithful ministry. I praise God for the privilege of having known him. His memory left a sweet fragrance. I count it a great privilege to have been in his circle of friends.'

Meanwhile the climax to the search for a new property was reached after three-and-a-half years. 'Bulstrode Mansion in Bulstrode Park has come to our notice. Had we seen this large property earlier I'm sure we would have turned it down flat, but God has been stretching us over these years and causing us to think of a new concept of headquarters life and ministry.

'Bulstrode is situated about eighteen miles from Marble Arch on the main road to Beaconsfield, High Wycombe and Oxford. It is about half a mile beyond the crossroads at Gerrards Cross, and approximately six miles north of Slough. It is ideally situated, being within twenty-five minutes of the airport by car, and has easy access to various motorways.

'If this property proves to be the one the Lord has for us we anticipate that the WEC Press from Kilcreggan and the Youth Crusade at present in Birmingham, will join us. They would be able to make use of the existing workshops and exploit the parkland. A brand-new warehouse which could hold about 1,000 people would make a good conference hall.

'There are still one or two planning committee meetings necessary before we receive the official permit, but we hope everything will be through and settled by about 16th January. After this we shall install our own caretaking party. Later a period of repairs and redecoration will begin.'

This time all went ahead, with God's hand clearly guiding and Len in his element organizing the great exodus, as he called the move. Once more it is Phil Booth who colours the picture for us. 'I well remember going over to look at Bulstrode before it was ours, when it was still in the hands of the previous owners. It was in a terrible state! It needed someone of Len's faith and vision to see how it could possibly be used. He just sat down and thought of all the various sections of the work that could be brought in and integrated. He began to feel out for lieutenants like Neil Rowe to handle the affairs. And in due course, the move took place. I don't know how much it is realized that although in a sense Bulstrode was put through administratively by Neil, really it is a momument to Len's faith. His was a faith that worked on the question of a new headquarters for some years, and eventually was able to rise to taking the terrific hodge-podge of buildings and accommodation Bulstrode was before it was all sorted out.'

Len's description is even more graphic: 'If you go round Bulstrode now you can die a variety of deaths—fractured skull on scaffolding, headlong fall into the basement, or there is a very fine death by suction in trying to help clear out the lily pond for fire-fighting resources!'

The great exodus eventually took place in October 1967. 'We actually began the move on Tuesday, 24th October and completed it on Tuesday the 31st. I rather enjoyed planning this move because it was like a young military operation. Personnel and baggage were sent on alternate days in order to give opportunities to settle in. We left one family in each house at Highland Road right to the last day as a safeguard against vandalism in any completely empty house. We estimated that we would need about eighteen pantechnicons to move everything, and so we asked for three per day. These were located at three different houses for loading, so that the men didn't hamper each other moving up and down the same stairway. Although it was a hectic period, and there can be no gainsaying that, things went fairly smoothly.

'Everybody was about dead beat with tiredness, and nearly everybody lost weight! But by the Lord's good grace and strength we have gone a long long way towards re-establishing WEC headquarters here at Bulstrode.'

And then, with so much going on, a crisis arose that same year in the Far East. Of course Len was needed. He flew off on 9th July, shedding the multitude of home interests and concerns and depending on the Lord for wisdom on how to advise when he reached his destination. He comments later, 'If all future negotiations are conducted with the grace, love and honesty with which these were conducted, there is nothing to be apprehensive about. Praise the Lord for his over-ruling love among us all.'

Six months later Len was off yet again. This time it was for a major six-month tour of South-East Asia with a couple of conferences included in his itinerary. The physical challenge of long months abroad, travelling from one country and culture to another and facing the demands of speaking, teaching, encouraging and advising, can only be met by the power of God's Spirit as a living, indwelling reality. Len not only lived in utter dependence on God's enabling, but as he travelled over the years he gleaned much information on the move of the Holy Spirit world-wide.

In January 1968 he left England for the long tour which was to thrill him, challenge him, and demand of him all the physical resources he could muster. The tour began in the Trucial States (Arabia), and from there Len went to Nepal where his niece, Margaret Owen, was a missionary nurse. Margaret says, 'It was great to entertain him in Pokhra where we shared fellowship in a boat on the lake. Len reassured me that God was well able to cope with anything he wanted to do through me. Len always expected Christians to wholly trust the Lord for everything, and he was a little impatient when he met hesitancy in anyone about following the Lord. He was always urging wholehearted commitment to the One who was wholly to be trusted. I thank the Lord for Len and for the fragrance he spread.'

It was clear that Margaret saw Jesus in her Uncle Len, and yet Len admitted that he did not always see Jesus in others. Speaking in America in 1973, Len was very honest about this. Referring to his visit to Nepal he comments, 'Do you know, I can be baptized in the Holy Spirit and full of the Holy Spirit, and yet Jesus can be

134

present without my recognizing him. If you want any proof, we read in the Bible that the Son of man says to the righteous, "Come in; welcome. I was sick and you visited me. I was hungry and you gave me food. I was in prison and you came to me." And the righteous say, "Lord, when were you sick? We never saw you in prison. When were you hungry?" He was there and they never recognized him.

'Have you ever seen Jesus sick? I have. I happened to visit a leprosarium in the heart of Nepal. And as I walked round that humble yet very efficient leprosy centre, I saw the tragic outcasts of Nepalese villages. This terrible disease was having its way with men and women and children. And I saw an overworked Christian staff trying to deal with this tremendous challenge. Thank God that there were those who were receiving a measure of healing, but the task seemed almost impossible.

'After I left that leprosarium, a dear friend of mine who is a pastor from England went to Nepal in order to have fellowship with missionaries. He flew in to the heart of Nepal and went to this very leprosy centre. And while he was there they had a very, very difficult case. There was one man sitting on the floor with his back to the wall. He was covered from head to foot with nodular leprosy, and it affected his understanding so that it was almost impossible to get anything through to him. Just a thin thread of life held that dear man from going over into eternity. The medical staff realized that they could do no more, and they asked whether this pastor would come and just pray over him.

'So the pastor said, "I'll pray if you'll tell him that I'm going to pray in the name of Jesus."

'"Hopeless," they said, "hopeless. We can hardly get through to him with the medicine he has to take. Talk to

135

him about Jesus and you praying to Jesus? Hopeless."

"'Please try."

'So this Christian nurse bent over and in the Nepali language said, "We are going to pray for you to Jesus. Pray—to Jesus. Do you understand?"

'And the man just looked blank. Not a scrap of recognition. She said, "I am sorry, sir, but we'll never get it through to him."

"'Try again."

"'All right. Look, we are going to pray for you. Pray. In the name of Jesus. Jesus. For you. Do you understand?" Turning to the visiting pastor, "Sir, we can't do it."

"'Excuse me, nurse. Will you try once more?"

"'Look. We are going to pray for you. Pray—for you. To Jesus. To Jesus—pray for you. Jesus."

"'That's enough," said the pastor. And laying his hands on that suffering body he just lifted his heart to the Lord and a stream of prayer went out, asking that God would come and do the miraculous in that body. Not only that he would bring healing power and love, but that into his heart might come the glorious light of salvation. And more than that, that the Holy Spirit might come into his life. This to a burnt-out leprosy case. The pastor just prayed that God would meet him. And he left.

'Healing began that very moment and, as far as I know, that man became a healthy man in whom has come an understanding of the Lord Jesus Christ.

'I didn't know then, but I know now, that I saw Jesus in those patients, Jesus sick. And I didn't recognize him. The pastor did.'

Moving on from Nepal, Len next visited Indonesia where the missionaries and the local Christians were seeking to come to a new working arrangement. 'There was to be a big conference and I was going to invite Indonesians to take their place in the Worldwide Evangelization Crusade as equal missionaries, so that we could present the whole church to the whole world. No more would it be a western organization going out to south-eastern countries. We would be international.

'I was eager for the time to be given me to speak in the conference. And I remember getting up and saying, "Dear Indonesian brothers, we want you to stand with us in world-wide evangelization. We invite you now to come and join us, not under us but with us, and pray God that we will serve together in the Crusade."

'I thought there would be smiles. I thought they would welcome this. I thought it was a privilege I was offering them. But I didn't see a smile. I saw no movement.

'That day was the 28th February, my birthday. All day the national leader, the assistant leader, the field leader and I discussed the situation, but there was no move at all. By tea time I was exhausted. I went for a walk in the garden and said, "Lord, I want a birthday present. Lord, please, please bring about an understanding and a spirit of love and fellowship among my three brothers. This has gone on for so long. We are at an impasse."

'The next day in the conference one of the Indonesians got up and said, "If Mr Moules is so concerned about presenting the whole church to the whole world, and that Indonesians join the Worldwide Evangelization Crusade, what hinders Mr Moules and his Crusaders from joining us instead of us joining them?"

'I rocked! Now the WEC was very, very dear to me. I loved the WEC. Ever since I finished my apprenticeship the WEC has been a dear friend to me. I went back to my room that night and you don't know the wrestlings that went on. But wrestlings there were.

'The Lord Jesus said to me by the Holy Spirit as I lay on my bed, "Len, you've been to many conferences in many countries, haven't you?"

"'Yes, Lord, I have."

"'What have you been teaching in these conferences?"

"'I suppose my main ministry has been Galatians 2:20, 'I am crucified with Christ: nevertheless I live; yet not I, but Christ liveth in me.'"

"'Yes, what else?"

"'Also that basically there's life out of death, and if we accept death then it's life to others."

"'That's right. And this is exactly what I want of you. I want WEC to die that it might live with life in others. Are you ready for this?"

'It was morning light before I said, "Yes, Lord, I'm ready for WEC to die."

'Later in the international leaders' conference we accepted that the ultimate destiny of WEC is to die in integration.

'I believe this to be the scriptural destiny of a mission. "Except a corn of wheat fall into the ground and die, it abideth alone: but if it die, it bringeth forth much fruit." The principle right through is that life comes out of death.'

At this time, and for a few years prior to Len's visit, revival had been spreading in Timor and the eastern island of Indonesia. Len writes, 'The very air had a spiritual tang. It was evident that God was moving significantly over the great necklace of islands, with the spiritual centre at the eastern end. The first lesson I learned was that God will do what he desires, through whom he desires, and when he desires, with such evidence of his power that he deems fit to manifest—and

138

he does not expect his people to enter into any controversy with him in these issues (Isaiah 45).

'The second lesson was very humbling and personal. I was co-chairman with Pak Peter Octavianus, Principal of the Indonesian Bible Institute, over a conference of 200 delegates from many areas and islands of Indonesia. Joining them were delegates from India—Brother Bakht Sing, Theodore Williams and Sarvanand Lal. From Germany came Dr Kurt Koch, already collecting valuable material for his book. From America and Britain came other mission and church leaders. During one of the reporting sessions Pak Peter Octavianus whispered to me that the next delegate would be one whom God had used recently to raise to life again two who had died. I was immediately alert, and anxious to meet and hear this testimony. I imagined a man of striking personality and authority. When the podium was vacant there was a long pause, and people began to wonder where the next delegate could be. Looking along the aisle I saw two men firmly but graciously propelling a reluctant, diminutive man to the front. There he stood, humble and retiring, radiant in the love and presence of the Holy Spirit. He thanked them for their prayers. God was doing great things in their midst and glorifying himself. He asked for their continued support in prayer as he returned to a new session of ministry. Then he sat down. Not a word of the mighty power of resurrection! The man was weak in personality but mighty in the presence of God.

'I eventually went to my room troubled. There God spoke to me. "Len, if I had done these mighty works through you, and you were in his place, would you have been reluctant to go to the front? Would you have omitted to speak of those mighty works in detail?"

'I had to admit that I would have been eager to be at the

front, and to have shared very early on how I had personally been involved in such miraculous events. Then God said, "Yes, you are right. But I can trust this dear Indonesian brother not to touch my glory." My prayer ever since has been, "Lord, thine is the glory, the honour and the majesty."'

Len's visit to Vietnam had to be cancelled owing to the political situation there, so he moved on to Singapore for another conference. Then he went to Thailand, where Iris met him so they could complete the tour together.

And then it was India. Len wrote with feeling, 'Imagine how it felt to walk up a familiar path after twelve years' absence, towards a smiling crowd of old fellow Crusaders and new ones we had never met. What a wonderful welcome to us both! We started off with a fine conference at which Leslie Brierley and Gerhard Bargen from Australia were present. I think all the WEC missionaries in India, except one couple, were there in full force. It was a great occasion and the fellowship was terrific.

'Then we left the conference and spent one week in our old hunting grounds in the Himalayas, and met so many old friends. It was a wonderful time. Tears flowed when we met those who have been so precious and dear to us, and it was a wrench to leave them and the places which hold such dear memories. To talk to them again was just an inspiration for praise and gratitude to the Lord for letting us return.'

The journey home took in Pakistan, Afghanistan, Iran, the Trucial States, Beirut and Istanbul; then back to London. Every place had its contacts, visits, business and interest.

Such was Len's first long tour. Like everything else it came to an end; the year continued with the round of duties, each refreshingly different, in the new surroundings at Bulstrode.

Len's secretary, Eileen Fowler, who held the reins in his absence, illustrates Len's care and consideration. 'As his secretary I came to know Len and Iris very closely, and our relationship was that of a team. It was often hard work, for Len set a good pace and I needed to keep up with him, but those years were some of the happiest of my life.

'His letters were very characteristic of the man, and his love and concern for the recipient were very evident. On one occasion he wrote to a couple who were planning a course of action which was felt to be wrong at that particular time. How Len pleaded as he put the other side to them! As I typed that letter I felt that had I been on the receiving end I would have been absolutely melted.

'On another occasion I found a draft letter among the pile of work Len had left for me. It was in reply to a rather difficult letter from an official of another society. Len's reply was very curt and almost stinging, and certainly not one that he would like to own. I was grieved in my spirit as I typed it. I left the office that evening with a heavy heart, and I ached before the Lord as I walked away. Next morning the letter was waiting for me—not signed and ready to be sent off as was the normal procedure, but crossed right through with the comment "God forgive me" written on it. I typed the new letter with a praising heart. Not a word passed between us about the original letter; nor have I ever told anyone of it until now. It was the only letter of that sort that I ever knew Len to write, and even that was scrapped. When he had to disagree or rebuke his letters were loving and gracious. If he erred it was on the side of love.'

CHAPTER NINE

PRAISES AND PRESSURES

By this time Len was attempting the impossible—to be both International Secretary of WEC and the British Home Base Leader at the same time. As his friend and close worker, Jack Aitken, comments, 'that was when the weight came on'. As no other nominee had been confirmed as the Lord's man for either task, Len carried the load cheerfully but with increasing physical weariness. But he gave a cry from the heart in one of his letters: 'The Lord has not yet shown to us our successors for British leadership, and we would commend this to you for prayer. Obviously it is beyond the ability of any couple to conscientiously fulfil the responsibilities of both the overseas and the British commitments, and both areas are suffering because of this. I am praying that either January or June, after the leaders' council, will give us clear direction as to the future. We do need to remember this in prayer.' Len wrote this from Tasmania in the middle of his second long tour.

Len writes of that trip, 'On 30th October I flew from London Airport on a six months' absence from Britain. This is a tour which will take me right round the world. Four months will be spent in Australasia, but already my time has included visits to America, Japan, Korea, Taiwan, Hong Kong, and Singapore. I plan to visit South Africa on my return journey and be back in the UK on the last day of April.'

From Singapore Len flew to Perth, Australia, to begin a four-month tour of that great continent. Everywhere he went all kinds of meetings were planned, and there was very little in the way of free time for rest and refreshment. One place reports that Len took twenty-nine meetings while he was with them! Len writes from Sydney, 'I'd love you to know that the high peak of the tour as regards its demands is now over, having had the heavy Thornleigh WEC convention and the Annual WEC staff meetings, followed by a further convention immediately afterwards. It has taken everything I had, and I'm pretty exhausted.'

And yet, two days after writing that Len took time out to send a card home to Mrs Dulce Martin, wife of 'Uncle Frank'. He wrote, 'Dearest Aunt Dulce, just a line to you to let you know you are never forgotten though I may be half-way round the world. The tour is half over and it has been mile by mile of blessing. Many souls have been blessed and others consecrated to a life of service. Last week was the Australian annual staff meetings. Many came with tears and apprehension, some with resignations; but all went away rejoicing and thrilled how God came into our midst and blessed us in a fellowship of love. The heavy part of the tour is over and I'm tired but God will refresh me, I know. Thank you for your prayers. Lots and lots of love, Len.'

The challenges were great and the demands never-ending, but every time God stepped in and supplied the need. 'They dropped me a clanger on Monday night by telling me that I was to go to Sydney in the morning for the first live broadcast of four, and then return at 2 p.m. to record three more programmes for the rest of the week. I thought it was to be done next week so I wasn't ready. All Monday night I was hard put to it, and I decided to take a series on "The most unforgettable characters I have met".

'On Wednesday I woke to find that I was booked to speak at the Prayer Day of Gospel Recordings and I knew nothing about it! I was told it would be a missionary talk and that I should give a world survey. This was at 8 a.m. and I was collected at 9 a.m. When we arrived someone remarked, "We're looking forward to this Bible study." Bible study! I had already prepared a missionary survey. So I thought, "Well, Lord, I must look to you." They gave me a very warm welcome and I began. I happened to mention how God was moving in the world and they said, "Tell us about it." I gave them a brief world survey for about twenty-five minutes, and then went on to speak on missionary vision from the last chapter of Deuteronomy.'

No wonder Len said on a personal tape, 'If I sound pretty tired, you've guessed right. One night I was not sure I could keep on. I feel mentally stretched at the moment.'

But there were those who tried to keep the pressures off. 'It was a great convention and well over two thousand attended at the peak period. The counselling that went on revealed the depth of the working of the Holy Spirit. It was a great privilege to be there. One sidelight: one day the chairman of the convention noticed how strained John Bird and I were with all the demands of the conference. On the day we were both free he packed us into the car and drove us into Melbourne. Do you know where he finished up? He put us into good seats to watch the Australia v. West Indies test match! Those four hours were a real break, and we returned to the spiritual test very much refreshed.'

The intention had been that Len should go on to New Zealand from Australia, but the best plans sometimes have to be jettisoned. Over in South Africa a number of problems had arisen which needed immediate attention, and Len was obliged to cancel his tour and fly direct to South Africa. Big decisions faced Len, and the Lord in his goodness prompted someone to spontaneously give Iris a gift which enabled her to fly out. Thus she was at Len's side to share the burden with him.

The problems centred round the Missionary Training College, and Len felt that the only way through the difficulties was to close the college at once. Two young missionaries, Ed and Aletta Markus, learned a valuable lesson about their International Secretary as a result of the incident.

'We were asked to meet Len at Johannesburg Airport when he was on his way from Australia to sort things out in South Africa. He greeted us and said he'd come to close the MTC; he had such negative thoughts about the whole situation. We saw him off to Durban soon afterwards. We were both shattered and shocked to think that he was going to close the college and didn't see any way of letting it stay open until the students graduated.

'A few days later we went again to the airport to see him for a short time while he was changing planes. I'll never forget it—it was just tremendous. That man of God came up and said, "I'm sorry, I was wrong in my attitude when I arrived here. We're not going to close the MTC. You are going to be able to have the students graduate."

'For that man in that situation of leadership to acknowledge he was wrong—and we were just accepted candidates! From that time, Len was to me a man of God. He humbled himself and then allowed God to direct his way. The graduation ceremony was so victorious and such a highlight.'

But others were hurt over the happenings at that time, and it was some time later that one wrote, 'For almost a year my heart was bitter towards you, Len. I knew it wasn't right, but try as I might I could find no room to forgive. But some months ago the Lord gave me real peace and removed all bitterness, and I want to say I hold nothing against you. I am truly sorry for having allowed the root of bitterness to spring up and defile me. I know God has forgiven. Praise his name!'

On the last day of April Len and Iris arrived back in Bulstrode, and immediately ahead lay a month-long leaders' conference. This was a daunting prospect to one who felt the load too heavy. After much consideration and prayer, Len and Iris sent the following letter to the leaders who were planning the agenda for the very full month that lay ahead.

WEC Bulstrode,
Gerrards Cross,
Bucks.
May, 1969.

Dear Leaders,

INTERNATIONAL SECRETARY

The purpose of this letter is to request consideration of a new appointment to the post of International Secretary. I regret to add further demands upon the Conference, but the reasons are as follows:

1. It is impossible for Iris and me to attempt to fulfil any further two appointments of British Home Base Leaders and International Secretaries. Neither task is being done satisfactorily, and it is beyond the ability of us both to

146

cope. Medical advice is clear that only one of the two appointments should be continued following this Leaders' Council.

2. It is an unwritten policy in WEC to see your successor in the visible before relinquishing your responsibility. For four years the British Staff have asked the Lord for His mind regarding our successors, and no word has been given. For two years now Britain has not had a leader touring the country in full representation of WEC and I feel it cannot continue any longer without loss to WEC in Britain.

3. My visits to Fields have confirmed to me that Iris should be with me. She has had a vital contribution which I could not give in fellowship with Field personnel and problems.

4. The ministry of the tour so recently completed was blessed of God. About 80% of those needing personal counselling were women. It is, to me, essential that Iris is with me in future, for obvious reasons.

5. Iris cannot leave home for extended periods for at least another three years. We are responsible for a daughter (14) who needs us now in a critical period of her life.

It therefore seems to Iris and me, after a long period of thought and prayer, that we should continue as British Leaders for a further elected period, subject to the approval of the British Staff.

If our successors could be duly considered under the discussion on the International Secretary, we would be most grateful.

Yours very sincerely,

Len and Iris.

WEC Leaders were coming from all over the world to be at the conference and Norman Grubb was to attend also. Perhaps it was the request he had made that caused

Len to feel some apprehension as the conference began: 'As I saw the delegates arrive I began to have butterflies in my stomach. As some wag said, my butterflies had marching boots on—they hurt! I had a wrong type of fear in my heart: fear of how the conference would go, fear that the delegates would eventually think it wasn't worthwhile coming, and lots of other satanic insinuations. And now I'm grovelling in sackcloth and ashes. It has been a month of terrific fellowship. The Lord has been in our midst. We sensed him walking among us. There have been times of brokenness and tears, many times of prayer, times of precious ministry, times of warm fellowship.'

At the close of the conference Len writes, 'The Crusade has come a long way in many things, and the fact that we could come through to unanimity on some of these issues is a precious expression that God is in our midst. The dimension of prayer and the sense of the Lord's presence in the leaders' conference make me feel that we've come down from the mount with the tablets in our hands. Not tablets of stone, but living policies for world-wide evangelization.'

And what about the resignation tendered by Len and Iris? Another letter went out, this time to British WEC staff and dated 3rd July. There was to be a change, but not the change Len and Iris had sought for before the conference.

Part of the letter reads, 'Naturally the letter of resignation Iris and I presented to the international leaders' council brought a new matter for discussion before the leaders' council, and we can say that a good deal of time was spent in prayer, discussion and inquiry. Unanimity did not come quickly but was finally reached, and the conference could authoritatively say it was the Lord's will for us to remain as International Secretaries. The resignation, not having been accepted, was withdrawn in the light of the Spirit's witness to us all.

'The future therefore does indicate a definite decision to lay down the British leadership. We will do so at this October staff conference in 1969. If all the above is in the Lord's will, as we know it is, then the Lord must be about to speak to us all regarding our successors. We stand together in fellowship to this end.'

At the close of the letter were listed several suggestions about Len and Iris's future,

SUGGESTED GUIDE LINES FOR
INTERNATIONAL SECRETARY
For remainder of Len's term (2 years)

1. We suggest that the matter of residence away from HQ but in the vicinity, be given serious consideration.
2. In view of recent tours and also the effect of this conference in the resolving of current problems, we do not feel extended overseas tours should be undertaken over the next two years, but short visits in line with his ministry should not be ruled out.
3. Greater care needs to be exercised in the matter of speaking engagements and membership of outside committees.
4. A yearly vacation of a few weeks' duration is considered essential.

LEADERS' CONFERENCE
Bulstrode, 1969.

The first of these suggestions eventually led to the ministry the Lord had planned for Len as the climax of his walk with the Lord. While living in Bulstrode, on the few occasions when Len was home, he and Iris had attended Gold Hill Baptist Church in Chalfont St. Peter. It was through this connection that Len and Iris were eventually granted accommodation in Graham House, a terrace of purpose-built living units attached to the church.

Some relief lay just ahead. After much prayer and seeking the Lord at the staff conference in October, Robert and Isabel Mackey were appointed as British Home Base Leaders. Len was released to move forward in his appointment as International Secretary.

Although Len intended to stay in Britain for some time, it was not possible to foresee situations in far-away places in which he would be needed. One such was a country closed to normal mission work, but which was willing for practical help once Len had travelled there to speak personally to the government officials.

Elwin Palmer of WEC USA tells us about another situation that arose: 'I was with Len on a delegation that went to one field in 1971. This field was a concern throughout WEC. It was felt that they were in danger of departing from some basic WEC principles, and we had to look into this and examine the situation carefully.

'I recall Len's stand on that occasion, and it was not an easy one to take. He knew he couldn't say, "this is what we've decided and you must live up to it." He didn't take that attitude, but he gave, nevertheless, a firm recommendation. He said that this was the way we as a delegation saw things; and "if you are prepared to accept this, good; if not, we will have to make our recommendation to the leaders' council, and their decision will be final." That wasn't accepted in just two or three minutes, but Len stood firm. Of course others of us on the delegation were praying for him and backed him up

150

None the less it was he as the leader who took a decisive stand, but in such a spirit that the others realized he was not giving an ultimatum. That characteristic made him the sort of leader he was.'

Despite these overseas trips, however, Len was busy in his office at Bulstrode for some months, keeping in touch with all that was going on.

One of Len and Iris's friends wrote, 'to know him was to love him.' That can be echoed by a multitude the world over, and especially by the young people he encouraged and loved and counselled. Lou Hayles was one of this number. She had been in great problems, to the extent that her life was in danger. When asked if Lou could come to Bulstrode, Len and Iris not only opened their doors to her, but also their hearts. Lou arrived in very modern, sexy clothes and was put in the care of Kip and Doreen Wear, a couple with a young family.

Lou says, 'Len was such an approachable man whom you could talk to. He was always so gracious that I never guessed he was so pressured. And he never said anything about the way I dressed. But while staying at Bulstrode I made a real commitment to Jesus Christ, and then I realized myself that I had to sort out my sexy clothes and cover my navel!' Lou described Len as 'a really beautiful man. I felt safe with him around.'

One other tour of Len's gave him an abundance of rich memories; this was when he visited West Africa from October 1971 to February 1972. The tour covered the Gambia, Senegal, and Ghana in the first two months.

Iris said in a letter written at the time, 'It was with special anticipation that Len faced Congo, now known as Zaire. It was going to be an opportunity to meet Africans who had worked with his big brother, Percy, who died of typhoid fever in 1944 at the age of forty-two.'

This part of Len's tour was packed with adventure as well as inspiration and interest. We have accounts of it from both Len and Colin Nicholas who, with Howard Burns, played a key part in Len's journeying. Speaking of that time later, Len says, 'I arrived in Zaire two days before Christmas Day. We put down at an airport called Kisangani. My French is very rusty, particularly when it's crackling over an aircraft intercom. I don't understand what they are saying but I see everybody get out, so I get out. Then they all get back in again, so I get back in again. The intercom crackles again and they all get out, so I get out; but this time they don't get back in and the plane takes off and I haven't reached the end of my journey. It is only forty-eight hours before Christmas Day, when I am due at a conference where some five thousand will gather.'

Colin Nicholas takes up the story. 'Len was due at Isoro for a conference which had been built round him, but his plane had engine trouble and put him down some three hundred and fifty miles short of his destination. There was no possibility of his getting there on his own so Howard Burns and I set off to fetch him.' Back to Len. 'On Christmas Day at 2.30 a.m. the telephone rang in my hotel room at Kisangani. It was Colin and Howard downstairs in reception. They had driven over eighteen hours on atrocious roads to rescue me. They were covered in red dust. The Land Rover carried a team of three boys from the school and ropes, planks, and shovels to help them get through. I dressed in my shorts and safari jacket and in the dark morning, at 3.15 a.m., we set out to drive the eighteen hours back. This was a baptism of Zaire! The terrors of the trip were Bailey bridges with no proper flooring, only two-inch bamboo poles laid loosely over the girders. It was really hectic, but Colin got the

152

Land Rover over well.'

Colin tells, 'The first three hundred miles were no problem, but after Niania it was very rough. What scared Len was a Bailey bridge fifty feet long with a drop of at least thirty feet to a fast-flowing river and not a plank on it—just the frame and poles from the forest laid across it! Howard went and spaced the poles, and Len got out saying that we should never have come! There were six other bridges that were just logs. Len's comment was that it was the worst journey he had ever experienced.'

Len says that by mid-afternoon they stopped in the Ituri forest. 'The road was like a corridor, with elephant grass on either side. But then we came to an intersection where a side road joined ours. I got out and looked down that road, because it was down there somewhere that Winnie Davies was killed twenty minutes or so before the National Army found her body.

'But out of that road also came a pastor. I met him. He had recovered somewhat from his ordeal of three-and-a-half years deep in the jungle. He told me that he had survived merely because they had met some pygmies and the pygmies had told them which leaves they could eat, which berries would give them strength and sustain them, and how to tap a tree for water. They learned from the pygmies where to find the minimum means of sustenance. There was a big group from the church that had had to hide deep in the Ituri Forest. And some in their midst had been traitors, and had leaked their whereabouts to others and they had had to go from one place to another, moving on all the time. The tension was terrific. The pastor said, "One of our dear brethren cracked mentally and became almost uncontrollable. What could we do? He was dangerous. We knew very little that we could do, but we were conscious of the Lord Jesus

Christ's presence by the Spirit every step of that jungle period. A few of us gathered round this mentally deranged man who was dangerous. Some held him while three of us laid hands on him and asked that there might be peace in the name of Jesus. The man relaxed, and peace came and mental balance was restored."

'A few months later a baby was dying of hunger, and it seemed as if the last hours had come. The pastor said, "the mother brought the child to us. In the name of Jesus hands were laid on the baby, right there in the heart of the Ituri Forest, and the Lord spared that little life."

'As I listened to him I felt almost unworthy to even touch his feet. He was a man who'd walked with God in these privations, a dear, beloved brother in the Lord, pastor of one of the churches.'

The welcome Len received was terrific. He describes the rest of that day: 'We arrived at Wamba in the last light to see Daisy Kingdon and Gladys Rusha, and had an overwhelming reception from the church. After half an hour we were on our way again. Howard was now down with malaria and Colin about dead beat after forty hours with no sleep, so I took the wheel for the last fifty miles. Night-time, headlights, a river ferry on canoes over the Poko, and not knowing the road. I revelled in it! Drove into Ibambi about 8.30 p.m., just as all the missionaries were sitting down to their Christmas evening meal. What a welcome—it was terrific! I guess 1,000 Africans appeared with lights and just mobbed me. Frank Cripps and Jack Scholes walked guard on either side to the church, as all insisted on seeing me. I was on view for half an hour, illuminated by petromaxes (a type of pressure lamp), and was hugged and hand-shaken until my thumb was numb. Then for a wash, a wonderful happy meal, and bed.

'From then on it was a very full programme. Up at 4.30 a.m., usually, with a meeting at 6.30 or 7 a.m. and another 10 a.m., and so the day went. Half an hour's message would take two hours with two interpreters, and sometimes three. By Thursday I was exhausted. The dust-laden air had sent a flu epidemic, and I caught it too and felt groggy.

'Twenty-four hours later I was standing in Wamba before 5,000 Africans. 5,000 of them! They couldn't get into the church, so they had built a palm-frond shelter.

'We were seated. Then the singing. As we were singing I noticed a table with a white cloth on it, and the bread and the wine for 5,000 partakers. It wasn't long before my hand was out for the bread to be put into it from African hands, as the church elders dispensed the elements from the Lord's table. A wonderful day!

'But the highlight, which I shall never forget, was the prayer session. At the end of the meeting they said, "We'll have a time of prayer." One man prayed, another two prayed. Three prayed. Four were standing praying. The Spirit of God was moving through in prayer, moving through in intercession. It was quite obvious that with 5,000 it couldn't go on like this. So the leader of the meeting said, under inspiration, "Let's all pray."

'And, dear ones, there were 5,000 people praying at once. It was like the roar of Niagara Falls as the sound swelled and rose and fell in that palm-frond auditorium.

'I was irreverent enough to have my eyes open. I had never heard or seen anything like this before. Was it sincere? Was it just something that had grown up with the church? There was a dear woman over here, praying as if she were the only one. A man there interceding with God as if he were alone in a field. What prayer! What prayer!'

In the middle of his West African visit Len was taken on tour for two weeks. During that time he fulfilled a desire of his heart. He tells us, 'WEC has one unique facet—it was born on the mission field. And I've been to the place where WEC was born. I was asked to get into a dug-out canoe in the heart of Africa, and I was paddled across the Lualaba River to the other bank. I was told that from there I would obtain a very fine panoramic view of the side where C. T. Studd eventually arrived with Alfred Buxton, the twenty-one-year-old youth, and where they put up their tent. At that spot WEC was born. It couldn't be seen on site because of the high elephant grass, but it could be seen from the far bank. Eventually the canoe grounded on the bank on the other side. I clambered out and ran up the steep path, and very soon I looked across the river. I saw the palm trees and the high grass, and immediately my thoughts went to mental images of those early days. And I just looked and looked and looked. My mind went back to this verse, "What shall I say? 'Father, save me from this hour'?"

'I suppose it must have been some three-and-a-half to four months previous to C.T. and the young man arriving in Central Africa that in a room in a house in south London, C.T. said goodbye to his wife. She was an invalid on the couch. When he said goodbye he had no knowledge at all when they would meet again. He was seventeen years in the Congo without returning, and he died. He wasn't ignorant of this possibility in moving out to the Congo because God, through Jesus Christ by the Holy Spirit, was asking this of him. He was a very sensitive man. He loved his wife. He had the same feelings as you or I, if we are married, have towards our wives—a deep love. Actually, I believe within forty-eight hours of his leaving, she took healing by faith, rose from that couch, and never went back to it. In fact, she walked the USA, Canada, Australia, South Africa, and New Zealand and with a fiery acclaim challenged young lives to join her husband away there in the heart of Africa.

'I wonder if C.T. ever thought when that battle was on, "What shall I say? 'Save me from this hour'?" If he had said, "I can't pay the price. I can't leave you, Priscilla. It's too much to ask. You're a sick woman. Already I am being criticized by church and friends. I think it's right for me to be beside you." Would there have been over 50,000 Africans Sunday by Sunday in later years worshipping a Lord Jesus Christ who is so dear and precious to them? But thank God, there was obedience. Thank God that C.T., no doubt with his wife in his arms at that farewell, said, "No, for this purpose I have come to this hour. Father, glorify thy name."

'This is the principle on which the Crusade was born. This is the principle by which it lives, I believe, day by day. Loving our lives we lose them. Hating our lives we find them.'

And brother Percy? Len had a tremendous welcome from those who remembered his brother. He was able to talk to them, and even see things that had belonged to Percy thirty years before. 'One man, now an evangelist, wore the last present he had received from Percy and Edith Moules, a cream-and-red-striped sweater. It was very precious to him and still as good as new, as it was only brought out on very special occasions!'

CHAPTER TEN

A MAN OF VISION

From the time when the Holy Spirit poured like liquid glory over Len, he was constantly gleaning information about the Spirit's outpouring round the world. He became not only a very able Bible expositor, but also an authority on the challenge to mission work in the future and on revival world-wide.

When writing on the latter for *His Paper,* Len said, 'It was early in 1973 that I had the privilege of fellowship with a dear brother from behind the Iron Curtain who opened up his heart with much praise to the Lord for the evidence of what God is doing in his country.' He went on to say that the moving of the Spirit in one town was so marked that attempts were made to prevent Christians from leaving the town. Eventually a member of the Politburo joined one of the Christian groups with the intention of studying the reason for the spread of these beliefs.

> During that time she was exposed to the tremendous power of the Gospel and her heart was touched and finally she became deeply convicted of her standing before God. This conviction led to a work of grace in her heart until she became a sincere believer and committed Christian.

There were many reports from Europe and Africa, Asia and Latin America. Len frequently spoke on these world revivals and brought encouragement to those who listened.

At the close of an article he wrote for *His Paper* on Colombia, Nicaragua, Korea, Ethiopia, Egypt, and Chile, Len said,

> Of the 210 countries which constitute the world scene, the stirrings of revival have now touched well over 70 countries since 1960. Behind the Iron and Bamboo curtains the Spirit of God is moving significantly.
>
> There are many lessons to learn from the decade of revival. Primarily it is the fact that God will pour out his Spirit when he wills, and through whom he wills. The manifestations of his outpourings are varied according to the will of the Reviver. Sometimes with mighty wonders and miracles; sometimes with sky-manifestations at night of a crown of thorns or the face of Jesus. Other times a deep wave of conviction leads to mass decisions and reconciliation or restitution. Revivals may come as earthquake or fire, or a mighty wind, but sometimes as a move of gentle stillness. No one will ever know what has triggered off many of these spiritual awakenings. Some obviously by earnest and persistent prayer. Others seem to have no such prelude, but are an act of the sovereign grace of God. The wide distribution of the Word of God has perhaps been the basis upon which the Spirit moved. But of it all we must say that God is greater and bigger than all our concepts of revival. We must learn to accept him through whoever he comes, and with whatever accompanying manifestations.
>
> What exciting days! Be ready, be praying, be expectant and thankful for revival that is at our door. Hallelujah!

In 1973 Len was at a missionary convention in Canada which was part of the WEC Jubilee celebrations in North America. He completed an incredible tour, leaving

London on 12th January and arriving back on 24th August. In those months he travelled 30,000 miles by air and 18,330 miles by road, and spoke at 246 meetings. From January to the end of March he went from place to place in the States, then to Canada, then back to the States where Iris met him for three weeks at Bethany Fellowship in Minneapolis. On 29th June Iris returned home and Len went on to South America, where he remained until his return to London and home at the end of August.

All the time he was giving out—teaching, counselling and advising. No wonder that his diary records increasing weariness as the tour proceeded.

Time and again Len records his times of prayer for those at home. When Iris had returned to England, Len wrote, 'Wrote Iris. Missing her so much. I love her dearly. Thank you, Lord, for giving me this wonderful precious life in such deep love and trust, and that we love each other so deeply and love you above all else.'

But all these pressures were not allowed to mar in any way his ministry to others. Speaking at Bethany Fellowship on that tour, Len challenged his listeners to think what they were saying, even in hymns. 'There's one verse of a hymn that it would not be right for me to sing:

> Prone to wander, Lord, I feel it,
> Prone to leave the God I love.

Do you know that verse? Honestly, I can't sing it. I've got no ''prone'' to leave the Lord. I love him. I love him so much. I love him tonight more than I've ever loved him before. And if any new aspect of my life is revealed, I just give it to him. Prone to wander? Don't mention the word.

'If I were to go back to my wife and say, ''Darling, prone to wander, dear I feel it, prone to leave you, wife I love . . .'', if I got a thick ear I'd deserve it! And if I won't say it to my wife, how can I say it to the Lord? It's not my experience.

'My experience is this, dear ones. When the Spirit of God came into my life, he gripped me and gave me a driving passion to see all God's purposes fulfilled in my life, even though I shall never understand why he in his mercy chose to reveal himself to me.'

With regard to the many separations and problems Len and Iris faced, Len must surely have been challenged by his own words at a missionary conference. 'If I were to ask you if you believed in the sovereignty of God, I'm sure you would say without hesitation, ''Of course we believe in the sovereignty of God. God has his hand in all affairs.''

'But let's narrow it right down. Do you believe in the sovereignty of God regarding your personal life? If you do, then this is what it means. It means that the next thing that touches you, whatever it is, is the best thing at the right time.'

Little did Len know how soon he was to be tested deeply about accepting God's sovereignty in a new way.

Arriving home physically exhausted on 24th August 1973, Len was only able to take a few brief days' rest before getting back into harness. But, though Len was eager in spirit and had so much to share, his heart could stand the strain no longer. On 3rd September Len had a severe coronary.

Everything had to be halted, but not for too long. As soon as possible Len and Iris went away on their own to Branscombe in Devon, to the holiday cottage of one of the elders at Gold Hill Baptist Church. By the time April came around again, Len was able to be involved in a four-day event called Missionary Concern. He not only chaired each evening rally, but also felt able to take a seminar each morning. As ever, there were those sections in his excellent teaching that stick in the mind:

'There's an adage which is absolutely true: you begin with a man, a man with a vision, a man of God. From the man you get a movement. Take our own society, WEC. God took up a man, C. T. Studd, a man filled with the Spirit for world-wide evangelization. Out of him came a movement. Now that movement grows, but what we're fighting is this—that a movement very often becomes a monument. This is a natural trend. Man, movement, monument. The humanism comes in, the flesh comes in, the Spirit fades. We go on, and we go on. We do all the works and the formality, but the life is not there. As somebody aptly said, "If God removed the Holy Spirit from the world today, 95% of Christian work would still go on."

'Think about it. This is the trend. You'll find that within one hundred years God raises up a man, a movement develops, then it seems as if the hard legal theology takes over, and hard legal theology nearly always quenches life. If I've got a choice, I'd far sooner have life than theology.'

Once Len was back in harness he recovered quickly. Early in 1974, a mere six months after his coronary, he climbed 3,000-foot Ben Arthur in Scotland.

As he moved towards full recovery much of Len's time was spent in study, in writing letters and articles, and in gradually taking up his ministry once again. He made it his job to keep in touch, whether it was with individuals or with new aspects of the move of God.

Dick Perfect, a close friend, shares the concern Len felt about people who were gathering for worship in homes instead of in churches. '"At many house-meetings," Len said, "they tend to develop an emphasis, generally on one or several of the gifts of the Spirit, and once you make an emphasis you are in error.

"'What these fellowships desperately need is the Bible-teaching ministry of the churches to balance them up. And the churches desperately need to be cracked open so that the ministry of the gifts can enrich them. They desperately need each other. I think we've got to marry the two together.'"

With less responsibility in WEC, Len and Iris were able to attend Gold Hill Baptist Church more frequently. Over the months God began to lead them to a new form of outreach. One of the suggestions for lifting Len's load as International Secretary had been that he and Iris might live 'away from the office'. It was at this time in 1974 that the flatlet in Graham House, connected to Gold Hill Church, was offered to them.

At the same time Len began to feel he was being directed to lay down his appointment at WEC and that something else, as yet unclear, lay ahead. The pastor at Gold Hill, the Rev James Graham recognized in Len a kindred spirit and a powerful preacher and teacher. Len was therefore invited to consider eldership at the Baptist Church. Len replied that he and Iris could well move away within a short while, and also that they felt they should know and be known by the fellowship to a deeper level before taking such a step. Len ends his letter to Jim, 'We feel that this may well be of the Lord as it is in your heart, but let it lie on our hearts quietly for a time. We shall certainly share with you anything that contributes to our future. At the moment a year's sabbatical rest seems essential to recharge the batteries before any new assignment.'

How right Len was—November found him in a hospital

in Northern Ireland with chest pains again, and he was given another warning to slow down. It was clearly time to lay down his position as International Secretary of WEC, but by no means could Len ever be persuaded simply to stop.

Iris sent a letter to their many faithful friends: 'With the laying down of International Secretaryship we are "grass-root WECcers" again, and through the thoughtfulness of WEC we are enjoying a "sabbatical" year. We will be at Bulstrode on Easter Monday with Len taking part in the ministry. In April we leave for eight weeks in the USA, accepting several invitations to renew fellowship and to have further ministry. The Kilcreggan WEC conference is in the diary for the middle weeks of August, so you can see that the year is not going to be inactive.'

So Len stood down from the position of International Secretary. The occasion was marked by an excellent 'This Is Your Life' put on by the Bulstrode staff in December of that year.

Writing in the WEC Annual Report for 1974, Robert Mackey expressed the feelings of the Crusaders: 'Our beloved Len and Iris Moules are bowing out after eighteen years of leadership at the home end—first as British and later as International Secretaries. Scarcely knowing how to express the warmth of appreciation we all feel for their leadership, ministry and unstinted service to WEC worldwide, I have chosen to quote the final paragraph of a letter drafted by Norman P. Grubb and signed by the delegates who attended the Consultative Council Conference in Kilcreggan this year:

We love you in Christ, we thank God for you with our whole hearts, and we know that your leaving of the International Secretaries' position is only the stepping-stone to some further vital commission among us in our great calling to 'the whole world for Jesus now'.

'Well done, Len and Iris! And may God bless you, and long spare you to be with us in whatever capacity he shall choose.'

One of the first ways in which God blessed through Len was in his ministry as a speaker at the Greater Pittsburgh Charismatic Conference in April 1975. Many thousands of people attended this conference. In complete contrast, on his return to England Len was privileged to escort one of the elderly WECcers, Miss Lilian Dennis, to a Royal Garden Party where 'Ma Denny's' work was honoured by Her Majesty. Because of Miss Dennis's physical disability Len was permitted to drive into the Palace yard, which pleased him immensely.

But Len did attempt to take things more slowly and to settle into the local church, and in the autumn of 1975 he agreed to serve as an elder of Gold Hill Baptist Church. Jim Graham tells how he saw the situation. 'Very rapidly he became part of Gold Hill, first of all as an elder. The marvellous thing about it was that it was the unanimous feeling of the elders at that time that it was right that he should join us in the leadership, and this was fully endorsed by the church. It was a tremendous encouragement to Len that it came through in a biblical way.

'Of course Len's value as an elder was impossible to assess. He brought so many qualities. He was a man of vision—possibly that was his big contribution—with the ability to see a way down the road ahead and also to be a kind of architect of the way ahead. Len could always see further than his contemporaries, and possibly his value was that he was prepared to settle for that. "That's where you are at the moment," he'd say, "but I tell you, that's where you are going. This is what will be." But there was no pushing and hassling and "let's get it done now". His attitude was, "If you don't think you can take a big step at this stage, let's take a wee step.'"

But this was the same Len in spite of the change of location. As ever, he was urgent about the need for prayer if anything was to be accomplished. Jim Graham very soon discovered this in a personal way: 'When he first joined us, after we got to know each other a bit better, I remember him sitting in my room very silently. He looked me up and down and said, "What priority has prayer in your ministry, Jim?" My initial reaction was to be offended that he did not know that I did pray and that I was a man of prayer, and yet that really challenged me. He wasn't asking me, did I pray? He was asking what priority prayer had in my ministry. I began to see that, yes, prayer had a place, but not the priority it demanded.

'I remember him saying several times when we were together that one of the first things we would discover, with amazement, when we got to heaven would be the important place of prayer, and what we'd missed.'

Later, when Jim and Len were working in close partnership, Jim discovered the diversity of Len's prayer life. 'I remember going in to him in his study one morning. He was sitting with a cup of coffee in one hand—he always kept a flask and a kettle and coffee near by—in his big swivel chair. He was facing the door when I came in. He looked to me as if he were staring into space, and I was aware I'd intruded. I said, "Sorry to bother you, Len."

'"Ah," he said, "that's all right. Come in, Jim. I was just chatting to the Lord." So incongruous, with the mug of coffee and sitting in the chair facing the door. The door wasn't locked. He was in another world. It was all so Len-ish, so normal.

'But Len could also be prostrate before the Lord, agonizing, pleading with the Lord: "Lord, I don't know how to talk to you about this, but we need a touch of power. I'm prostrate before you. We need to hear what you have to say to us." And the other way was sitting with the cup of coffee. But it wasn't "either or"; it was "both and". And presumably in many other ways as well.'

So began a rich, even crowning, ministry which lasted until the Lord took Len to himself.

Len's next opportunity for ministry further afield was at the Kelham Clinic in the summer of 1976. By this time he had become a grandfather twice over; all three of the family had married, and Noel and Beth had each presented Len and Iris with a granddaughter that year.

At Kelham Len spoke powerfully on the biblical fusion of the word of God and the power of the Spirit as necessary for the blessing of God: 'From cover to cover of the word of God I find that God begins to move when word and Spirit are fused. At creation we have the record that the Spirit was moving over the face of the waters. Then, as the Spirit was moving "God said, 'Let there be light'; and there was light." The word came as the Spirit was waiting.

'We find that even in the birth of our Lord, the word and the Spirit fused together. The angel said to Mary in Luke 1:35, "The Holy Spirit will come upon you, and the power of the Most High will overshadow you; therefore the child to be born will be called holy, the Son of God." The Spirit was there, resting upon the instrument that God was going to use for the coming of the Redeemer. "And Mary said, 'Behold, I am the handmaid of the

Lord; let it be to me according to your word.' "

'You seem to get the Spirit waiting for the word. And when the word and the Spirit meet you see the manifestation of the power of God in the purpose of that time.

'I have been involved in Christian work at many levels since the age of twenty-one. As I look back over those years of Christian work, I come to the conclusion that I dare not, we dare not, move in any ministry of the church unless we know that Spirit and word have touched us and we're moving out with them burning within us. This is proved by the results; when God's in a thing you know it. You see God-like results coming from it.

'If the Holy Spirit were removed much work would go on, because it has been only word-motivated. In the past this has happened. So much missionary work needs to be re-examined by dedicated personnel. Too often we look around and say, "Our Lord healed, so we'll heal. Our Lord taught, so we must give education." But the Lord has taken us apart and shown us that so often Jesus said, "What do you want me to do for you?" Jesus moves in at the point of need. And when the need is met, things happen.

'Let's have the word but wait for the Spirit.'

This powerful teaching made Len's ministry all the more real and relevant. While at Kelham he also talked of the problem the Pharisees had where Jesus was concerned, and brought it home to the church of today.

'I would imagine that on the Temple notice board in those days there was a poster which went something like this:

WANTED: JESUS CHRIST

Other names: Messiah, Son of God, King of kings, Lord of lords, Prince of peace. Notorious leader of underground liberation movement.

Wanted for the following charges:

Practising medicine.

Wine-making.

Food distribution without a licence.

Interfering with the business of the Temple.

Associating with known criminals, radicals, prostitutes and street people.

Claiming to have authority to make people God's children.

Description

Typical hippy type; long hair, beard, Roman sandals.

Hangs around slum areas. Sneaks out into the desert.

Has a few rich friends.

Beware!

This man is extremely dangerous.

His insidious, inflammatory message is particularly dangerous to young people who haven't yet been taught to ignore him.

He changes men and women and claims to set them free.

Warning!

Jesus Christ is still at large.'

'Bless God, he is!

'It's in the church that we are going to have our problems. I remember being in a church when a group of hippies came in, and you could feel the atmosphere change. You could almost see the church wrap its cloak around it. The mandate of Christ is that we move to all with the love of Christ, no matter who they are.'

To this end Len and Iris, together with Jim Graham and his wife Anne, were praying. Len declared their commitment and intentions to those gathered at Kelham: 'I'm going back to my pastor and we're going back to our knees, because we are dissatisfied with the impotence we feel. And this is going to be until the Spirit of God falls on us as a church. And then we can look out to the

169

problems in the area where we work. God has already begun to work, but we're impotent at the moment.'

Len finished his talk at the Kelham Clinic with a cry from the heart. 'What can I say? Dear ones, I believe that if the church of Jesus Christ in this country were to but try the means God has given us by the Holy Spirit, many of the problems we face would disappear. If we were Spirit-filled and Spirit-anointed and Bible-based and moving in the will and purpose of God, no doubt it would be a different picture entirely. Have we tried the means?'

During this time of seeking after God, Len and Iris took yet another vital step in their lives. They describe this in a letter to their friends. 'No doubt the major change in the direction of our lives occurred on our return from the WEC Kilcreggan conference at the end of August. It was significant that the engagements for 1977 had been very few indeed compared to previous years at that point. And we had never before been engaged in so much counselling as we experienced from August onwards, as needy people came for spiritual help and guidance.

'So on 1st October we officially retired from WEC, but still maintain a close fellowship with them. On 1st November Len was recognized as associate pastor (at Gold Hill) and is being commended by the elders and church this weekend, 5th December. Do please pray for us in this thrilling new ministry.'

The ministry of counselling was to play a major part in the coming months. Len was in every way a practical man: physically, in tackling mountain peaks; materially, in the endless production of useful gadgets for car or kitchen; and spiritually, in that he acted on what he believed. He brought this practical emphasis to bear on his ministry. Jim Graham gives a graphic description of one occasion:

'I remember seeing Len in my study one morning when I'd jerked my neck while I was washing. Len said, "Good morning. How are you this morning?"

'And I replied, "Fine!" but with my head all taut.

'He asked, "What's the matter with you?"

'"I jerked my neck when I was drying myself this morning."

'"Oh. Well, you can't go through the day like that. You need prayer."

'"I'd really appreciate that, Len."

'"Right," he said, "Kneel there." (I keep a kneeler by my desk.) "Take off your tie and loosen up your shirt."

I thought, what in the world . . .?

'"Where's the oil?"

'"Behind the curtain."

'"That's fine. Right."

'He emptied some oil onto his hand and began to massage away at my neck with the other hand raised, praying away, "Lord, just bless this brother. He's really hurt his neck. Lord, as we apply this oil. . . ." He was rubbing away. It was this lovely combination of the practical and the spiritual, the word at work through a man. There was such a matter-of-factness.

'After it was over it was straight on to work, not, "Is it better?" He'd prayed, he'd rubbed in oil, and now let's get on with it.'

Counselling and meeting people's deep needs through the power of the Holy Spirit was every bit as important to Len as taking the place of teacher and preacher at a great convention.

He once said, 'When opportunities arise we work and slave and slave and work. But have we got our priorities right? The Lord said, "By this shall all men know you are my disciples, if you have love one for another." The mandate of Christ is that we move to all with the love of Christ, no matter who they are."

Len very honestly brought his own life into focus to show how God will use our failures if they are given to him. 'You are going to be helped when testimony is given to the grace and strength and love of God coming through in someone's failures, maybe just as much as by a testimony that's given of how God moved very positively in someone's life. God even makes our failures redemptive, and I think that's tremendous.

'When I look back on my own life there are things I'd love to forget, but I can't. There are lots of things I should remember and don't. And I think, "Lord, why can't I forget this?" But no, it comes back with regularity and just sobers me. The Lord says, "I know this was a lesson to you, but I want you now to make it positive to someone else." Time and time again I've sat with young men as they've shared their problems and areas of indiscipline in their lives, and the Lord has said, "Now you can share with them." What was such a grief and tears to me years back, I now see redemptively being made life to others as I share it. And so our failures that have been such a grief to us can become a glory to others. But it costs something, doesn't it? This is where the cross comes in.

'You don't know the battles that go on in my life. You don't know the mental engagements I daily have with the enemy. It's a battle. We're moving on in this battle, and any man or woman who has committed his or her life to God and is in the will of God, is a target of the enemy. Remember that. You are on his mailing list. He's watching you and accusing you, firing arrows that would wound you. He wants to remove you from the will of God. You are very important. The battle's unrelenting, it's on and on and on. The enemy wants to know, where is your weak point? Where is the undisciplined area in your life? If he can get to know it, that's where the pressure goes on.

'There is no spirit of experience that gives you discipline. Get that straight. You can go up to a penitent's bench a hundred, a thousand times. There is no spirit of experience that makes you come in an undisciplined person and go out a disciplined person. What happens is that the Spirit of God comes into your life to assist you in coming to grips with this matter of discipline.

'There are two ways of facing temptation. When you can't flee you trust in the grace of God. When you can flee, then it's up to you to get out of it.

'As far as we have the authority and the power to decide we should not go into those areas, keep those acquaintances, or make those associations from which we have been delivered once and for all. They are out! "Come out from among them and be separate." Those roads are never to be walked again. Those associations are never to be made again. God didn't deliver you to allow you to go back and tempt his providence near those experiences again. God expects you to keep clear.'

Jim Graham says that 'Len was a man's man, very rugged, and yet he had a tenderness that was very moving. I've known him give very strong corrective counselling and, having done it, to weep when the counsellee has gone because of the hurt that might have been caused.'

One of the great joys of Jim Graham's ministry was the Lord's provision of a co-worker of the calibre of Len Moules. Many men of experience would have found it

173

difficult not to step in and take over, even expecting Jim to respect and give place to them as the older man. But that was not Len. Jim speaks glowingly of their working relationship: 'Len was a man who had authority because he accepted authority. I think I saw that in his relationship with myself. So far as Len was concerned I was the leader, although there was no way I could even approximate to his leadership. I knew that, but I don't think he ever did. There was such a genuineness about that. He said regularly, "I am here to confirm and support you in the ministry God has given you."

'Here was a man who'd travelled the world for forty years, who had entered into the secrets of blessing, who had experience and a vision that I never had. But Len would agree that leadership is in a sense a purely functional thing. There must be leadership to keep things moving forward in order, but status in the Christian life is settled at the cross. Len felt that very deeply.'

Len entered into the life of Gold Hill and wholeheartedly carried his share of pastoral duties. But he did not in any way withdraw from the many other commitments that were part of his life. Besides requests to speak in many places, Len still sat on many committees and still lectured the young, up-and-coming missionaries. Iain and Margaret MacKenzie, Candidate Secretaries of WEC, speak of his last series of lectures to WEC candidates: 'Without question, there was still the same restless Len—restless for more of God, restless for deeper understanding of God's ways in the world, restless to sift out what it was that God was doing in his world. He covered in some six hours the expansion of the early church, right through a historic approach to missions to the present-day situation where indigenous churches are grasping the apostolic vision of mission.

Len always saw the bigness of God at work: I suppose he refused to see his God as being too small.'

It was impossible to slow Len down or to treat him as a sick man. In fact, the letter sent out by Len and Iris at the commencement of the co-pastorate states, 'The church desires that we keep up our missionary contacts and experiences, so for two months a year we hope to have overseas contacts. And we shall be in Indonesia for June and July at the invitation of the Batu Fellowship, no doubt touching the Far East and the USA on our return in August 1977.'

CHAPTER ELEVEN

ALL AUTHORITY

'If I were a missionary again, I would seek the Lord through a new life of prayer,' Len had once declared. Through the years that life of prayer did develop and became a way of life.

'If I were a missionary again, I would go back with a new personality.' Len developed that new personality as he learned to live in Galatians 2:20. At the thanksgiving service for Len's life, Jim Graham paid tribute in these words: 'I have lost a loyal friend, a co-worker in the gospel, and a dear prayer partner. Only eternity itself will be sufficient to record what God did through his servant, his son and his soldier, Len Moules. Having shared a little part of his life, I know that the crucial scripture that sums it up is Galatians 2:20. Anything that has been said or will be said about Len Moules centres on this reality. To see that is to understand; to miss it is to misunderstand.'

Len had declared a third area of change: 'If I were a missionary again, I would wish to know more of the authority of the Lord Jesus Christ in all the situations which challenged me. I can humbly say that by the grace of God and by the coming of his Holy Spirit since that time I know a little of that authority.'

Len and Iris visited Indonesia in the summer of 1977, and Len sums up the challenge there by saying, 'Indonesia is a continent of spiritism. In fact, they call the government's five-point programme "The Five Spirits". You face it on every hand.

'Those of us who go out to confront the enemy in his own kingdom have got to go out with an authority that is greater than the devil's authority. At the name of Jesus the devil must let go those whom he holds, at Jesus' command.'

Len tells of many wonderful miracles, of dreams and visions and healings that had taken place in recent years. He asks, 'What would Indonesia teach me this time?', and continues, 'In the eastern area of Indonesia the revival had matured into a deepening of the spiritual life of the church. There had been a quickening among both Christians and unbelievers, but the spectacular manifestations of the Spirit had almost ceased. Yet the church knew the power of God to heal and was constantly seeing the deliverance of those possessed by evil spirits.'

Back in England, Len was actively engaged in that same ministry of deliverance. He warned, 'More and more we are finding that people are taking to the occult. I understand there are somewhere around three hundred thousand covens of magic rites which are practising openly in Britain today.

'We have white magic, where symbols and hymns and even the terminology of the Trinity are used. Although they say they only act magically for the good of mankind, nevertheless it is demonic.

'There is black magic where the witch is given entirely over to satanic control, satan worship.

'We've got spiritism today. Men and women are

dabbling in it here every bit as much as in far-away countries.

'And we have something which people are regarding lightly but which has a devilish influence, called the ouija board. This ouija board has been sold by the thousand upon thousand, and there is hardly a school in Britain where it has not had some part between morning and afternoon sessions. We have stories of Christian children who have gone to see what it was, and have been struck by terror and run all the way home to the security of Mum or Dad.

'I regret to say that there is an incursion of the demonic into the lives of those who enquire or practise in these dimensions. I want to underline this. We find candidates who share about spiritual darkness and spiritual bondage. They are unable to contribute in prayer and testimony, and sometimes nights become nights of terror for them. This eventually comes to our knowledge, and as we seek to counsel them we go right back to early days: attitude to father and mother, attitude in the home, where they have been, and so forth. As their life is put through the sieve of questioning, if we find that they have dabbled personally at any level of magic or ouija board, or that their mother or grand-mother has been a spiritist medium, then there has been an incursion of the demonic into the personality.

'I want to be absolutely clear here. When I talk like that I don't mean demonic possession. Cases of demonic possession, when a person has no control whatsoever over what he is doing or saying during a given period under that possession, really are few and far between. But we have an increasing number of cases where people have been dabbling with the demonic, and there has been an incursion of the demonic into the emotional or the physical realm. Of course there is demonic oppression, which is outside, but you can also get a demonic incursion at this level of body, soul or spirit.

'Dear ones, today, as we go out in our missionary responsibility we're going to face demonic incursion in white magic, in black magic, in the horoscope, and in spiritism. I plead with you, don't touch these things. As we face the demonic we've got to have the authority to be able to deliver those who have been touched and affected by it.

'The devil's kingdom is the same all the world over. But now I could say, "Lord, you, with all authority, are with us. Lord, glorify your name."'

That tour to Indonesia in '77 saw renewed friendships, refreshed memories, and contacts made. Len and Iris met Margaret Hollands in Kuala Lumpur and Karen Druliner in Manila, both from Gold Hill Baptist Church and serving with the Overseas Missionary Fellowship. WECcers greeted Len and Iris at numerous places. At Semerang in mid-Java, some Bethany Fellowship missionaries whom Len and Iris had known for years appreciated the help and counsel they received through the visit.

'A few days were spent in Anaheim (California) at Dr Ralph Wilkerson's Melody Center, staying with our dear friends Vic and Jan Ramsey of the New Life Foundation. And what a thrill it was to arrive in Albuquerque and meet Bus and Marge Williams again, and all the dear friends at the Christian Center! We touched down at Houston to snatch a day with Mike and Linda Storey, who were with us in Gold Hill. Finally we burst in on the WEC conference in Camp Hill, Pennsylvania. So many of our North American colleagues were there, and it was terrific to be with them. On the 24th August, tired, weary

179

and rejoicing, we boarded the "jumbo" for home.

'Surprise of surprises was to be met by our daughter Carol and her husband Peter; they had come down from Birmingham. It was lovely to have this welcome home. Our other daughter, Beth, had a meal ready in the flat. Soon the wires were humming as we contacted the rest of the family. God has truly knit us together with real love. Beth and Bill are expecting a second baby any time. Our two grandchildren are tops!'

This was to be Len's last trip abroad. His programme gathered speed immediately on his return. 'The love and ministry of Gold Hill soon enveloped us, and we have been very busy—too busy—ever since. There was a real period of getting over jet lag. Len was hit first and recovered; then Iris, and she has taken much longer.

'The Lord has blessed the church life. It has grown to such a degree that we must look deeply at the caring ministry, which is breaking under the strain. Do pray that we may know his guidance in all things. We are both engaged in much counselling, but there is so much to encourage.'

Picking up where he had left off in May, Len began to fill engagements and carry the pastoral duties as before. But in September, shortly after his return home, 'God sent a man with a message to me and he said, "Len, I'm from God and I have a message for you. Unless you get away with God in fellowship with him, for a relationship with him and for an anointing on your ministry, you'll be a blunt axe. You'll labour and work and be tired and the trees will not come down. But if you will come aside with God he'll sharpen that axe and give you that anointing. And as you move out into his ministry those trees will come down, and daylight will come through where there has been darkness."

'Now, you can't turn your back when God sends a man many, many miles, a man of God, to say a thing like that to you. And, dear ones, I have got to come to terms with this. I have come to the end of a very, very full programme wondering whether I could make the evening of each day, absolutely exhausted and just longing for Monday morning, because the programme from Monday onwards had not got the pressure. But Iris and I have got to look at that programme, and we've got to see where those times are to be found. I know there will be a knock on the pastoral office door. I know the phone will ring. I know we've got to get off that patch and get away with God.'

But how? That was Len's problem. He was willing and eager to obey, but the church was there and needed to be led. The diary was filled with meetings, week after week right through the winter and scattered through the months of 1978. He had so much to give, so much to share, so much of value to impart to God's people—so many precious things.

Perhaps one message Len would want to leave would be on the five precious things the apostolic church had come to know by the time John was writing the Revelation. 'The first precious thing is that salvation is by faith in the precious blood of the Lord Jesus Christ, who died and rose again, who is Son of God and is seated at the right hand of God the Father in heaven.

'The second precious thing is that the Holy Spirit is central in the authority of the church.

'The third precious thing is this; that the divine word of God is the final authority in all matters of faith and conduct.

'The fourth precious thing is the priesthood of all believers.

181

'And the fifth precious thing is that fellowship is in the Spirit.

'Now, these are the five precious things which evolved as the Spirit, through the apostles, taught that church. But within four hundred years the church had lost them all.

'Salvation was by church membership and the sacraments.

'Ecclesiastical authority was the centre of the church.

'Tradition took the place of the Bible as the final authority.

'The priesthood of all believers was lost and was confined to a select few.

'And fellowship was in doctrine, and not in Spirit.

'We lost all that God had given us and went into a thousand years of darkness. But remember this; God never allows the darkness to be unbroken. He loves to have a remnant—a remnant for revival, a remnant for remembrance, a remnant for himself.

'And then God looked down, (we don't know why, though we will one day) and said that the time had come when he would give back the things we had lost. Bless the Lord, there's a restoration of all that we lost and of all God gave to the apostolic church.

'I know, dear ones, that we are denominationally-minded. I think it would be good for us to remember that when a denomination came into being it had a spiritual truth which the established church would not allow. People came out to enjoy that truth, and as a cross and a serpent were raised in the wilderness for the purpose of healing, I believe that the denominations came out for a purpose in that day. But that brazen serpent eventually became a thing to be worshipped, and it had to be destroyed. Its usefulness was finished. Please don't take

182

me wrong, but I do believe that today the denomination has to decrease and the body of Christ has to increase. Across the barriers, heart has got to go out to heart in love and joy and praise.

'We're in a day when it's the word and the Spirit. If we were to examine our hearts we'd find that there are few of us in balance. We're long on the word and short on the Spirit, or long on the Spirit and short on the word.

'May I say a word to those who hold the word of God very precious? You've read the word and you know the word, and in the word there is victorious life in Christ Jesus; but you are not enjoying it. In the word there is joy, but you don't know it. In the word there is victory, and you don't know even the name of it. In the word there is a relationship such that I am in Christ and Christ is in me; but as far as you're concerned, it is just the word and not an experience. Dear ones, you know the word and you acknowledge the word and its truth; but as for your experience, no! What's lacking? Spirit. Oh, may the Spirit of God come upon you dear ones! Let the word and the Spirit together make a person filled with the Holy Spirit in worship and love and joy and praise, in a victorious life and a relationship with the Lord God himself that you've never, never known before.

'There are those of you, no doubt, who are long on the Spirit. You've hungered after the gifts. You enjoy the gifts. You're never more thrilled than when your hands are raised in worship and love and praise and your feet are dancing. This is tremendous. But how about the word? Dear ones, if it's Spirit without word it can be tragedy. Word without Spirit is disaster. Spirit without word is tragedy.

'God wants us to be moving in the dynamics of the Holy Spirit balanced by the word of God. May we make a

resolution that the lack of our life may be made good,
that we may go out men and women of the word and of
the Spirit, because this age desperately needs it.'

CHAPTER TWELVE

ON TO THE SUMMIT

'In 1978 many things will change, but there are four that will never change: my Saviour, my assurance of him, my experience of him, and my eternal destiny with him. Is there a young man or a young woman who will say, "I'll take the torch and I'll follow on. My life will be poured out to bring back the King and establish the kingdom of God on earth as it is in heaven"?' That is how Len concluded his New Year message on the first Sunday of 1978.

But Len was not handing on the torch in order to bow out and leave the stage to others. Len, with Iris, Anne and Jim Graham, was still prostrating himself in prayer that wisdom might be granted for Gold Hill church through 1978 and beyond. The church was growing and new friends were coming, drawn by the love, joy, and general care shown by the church family for each other and the people they met in the street, the shops, the hospital.

A way of coping with this increase in the church life and the weight of responsibility in ministry at all levels was needed. The plan for Gold Hill became clear in those times of prayer. The revelation given to Len was for a restructuring of the leadership of the church in order to spread the load. This would mean an enlarged full-time pastoral team, greater responsibility for the part-time elders, and deep personal care among house-group members.

Jim Graham tells us what eventually took place: 'The blueprint for the future was totally accepted at one of the most thrilling church meetings I've been to. It was Len's birthday, but he wasn't there; he was ill. What happened subsequently was that instead of increasing the leadership in the church, the Lord decreased it. We had an eldership of ten and thought we'd move up to fourteen or fifteen. But none of those nominated was appointed and two of the original elders were eliminated, so we were reduced to seven. And by that time Len had gone to glory.

'It was always a great thrill to Len to see the Lord doing it in his own way. As if God said, ''That's the way you thought it would be done and I'm going to do it, but I'm not going to do it your way.'' That was so much in character with Len, I'm sure he would have loved it!

'The burdens on a person like myself were pretty heavy, because the resources were reduced. First we lost Len and then we had a reduced number of people to work alongside, but the year was tremendous. What the Lord did was to knit the present elders into such a closeness of fellowship that it was beautiful. It had to be a Gideon's band, greatly reduced, in order to make us feel our tremendous need for one another.'

At the time, Len himself was perhaps the only one who realized that he might not be working in that Gideon's band. But Len's commitment to his Lord and Saviour was to go on, always to go on. Speaking at Bethany Fellowship a few years earlier, Len had said, 'I would love to be able to say at the end of my life, "I have fought the fight, I have kept the faith," and to know that there is laid up for me a crown of righteousness.

'And no doubt each one of you without exception feels what I feel tonight. To come to journey's end, to come to the end of the fight, to come to that point when you know it's not going to be long now before you are in the presence of your precious Lord and Saviour; and to be able to say, "I've fought the fight, I've run the race, I've kept the faith." We all want to say it, don't we? We want those to be the last words we are known to have said before we go on into the Master's presence.

'But, dear ones, there is one thing I want to underline this evening. You won't be able to say, "I've fought the fight," unless you are fighting tonight. You won't be able to say "I've kept the faith," unless you are keeping the faith tonight. You won't be able to say, "I've run the race," unless you're running the race tonight. No man can come to the end of a life of self-centredness and ease, a life in which the will of God has been secondary to his own will, and hope to be able to say in his last breath that he's fought the fight, he's run the race, he's kept the faith. You can't do it.

'You only say in the last day what you are living today. If you're fighting today, you'll have fought the fight then. If you're running today, you'll have run the race then. If you're keeping the faith today, you'll be keeping the faith then. If you want the privilege of leaving a final testimony lingering in the ears of mankind, you will gain it only because you are fighting tonight, keeping the faith tonight, running the race tonight.'

Len knew that his days were nearly over. He had another slight coronary in February 1978. At one of the last Gold Hill staff meetings that he attended, he commented, 'I recognize that Paul said, "I have learned how to abound and how to be abased" and how to be content, but I find it so hard to be content with this bodily weakness.'

Afterwards Len sent Robert Mackey, International Secretary of WEC, an envelope on which he had written, 'Gather up the fragments that remain.' Inside were several smaller envelopes containing banknotes from the various countries he had visited. He was aware that his travelling days were nearly over: he would not need those notes again.

But Len was ready for the next journey he faced, to his beloved Lord. He once told fellow missionaries, 'I have written in my Bible as a constant challenge some words taken from *Pilgrim's Progress*. Mr Valiant-for-truth says, "I am going to my Father and, though with great difficulty I got hither, yet now I do not repent me of the trouble I have been to arrive where I am. My sword I give to him who succeeds me in my pilgrimage, my courage and my skill I give to him who can come and get it, but my marks and my scars I carry with me to be a witness for me that I have fought these battles for the one who will now be my Rewarder."'

Len had perhaps only one fear where meeting his Lord was concerned, and again it centres on prayer. 'When I get to glory what I'm fearful of is when the Lord tells me, "I am omnipotent. I could have done all things, if only you had cried to me. I wanted to do them, but you never came. I know there were many impediments. You asked, but I had to wait until you sought. You asked and sought, but I had to wait until you knocked. If you'd only knocked I would have moved on your behalf. But you didn't. And it's too late now. Your lifespan is gone."

'"Lord, if I'd only known."'

188

But Len did ask, Len did seek, and Len did knock. He was always reaching higher, always heading for the top.

Robert Mackey sums it up, 'Mountaineering was in Len's blood. He was never satisfied except when climbing.

> Bring me higher, nothing dreading,
> In the race that has no stop.
> In Thy footsteps keep me treading,
> Give me grace to reach the top.

> God did just that.
> On 17th March 1978, Len reached his summit.'

In a tribute to his father at the thanksgiving service for Len's life, Noel Moules leaves the future in our hands: 'The life of the Spirit of God has no end. This is just a transition. For us it is a time to stop and give thanks and take stock of ourselves. And for Dad, it's glory. Tremendous!

'In the ancient world, when a warrior died he was wrapped in his cloak, and his sword and shield and spear were buried with him. The only cloak that wraps Dad this afternoon is the cloak of the mystery of the glory of God, and he has handed on to us those weapons that were for the building of the kingdom of God.

'Dad was a man of the kingdom. He is one example of what can begin to happen when flesh and blood are ignited by the Spirit of God. Dad would have us do nothing else than pause a little, and then go into what he was going into—that is, bringing back the King and establishing God's rule of peace in this world.

'There's no more to say other than, let's be up and doing.'